SWING TRADING FOR BEGINNERS:

The Simple Guide with Secret Strategies to Trade Stocks, ETFs, Options, Futures, Currencies and Cryptocurrencies. Make a Living and Create a Passive Income from Home.

Introduction *1*

Chapter 1: Swing Trading Basics *13*

Chapter 2: Characteristics of A Swing Trader *43*

Chapter 3: Swing Trading Market Characteristics . *49*

Chapter 4: Finding a Suitable Market *67*

Chapter 5: Tools for Every Beginner *83*

Chapter 6: Fundamental Analysis *101*

Chapter 7: The Psychology of a Successful Swing Trader *108*

Chapter 8: Money Management *116*

Chapter 9: Risk and Account Management *143*

Conclusion *153*

Introduction

There are different trading styles and strategies used by traders around the world. These are often used based mostly on preference. There are traders who thrive on particular strategies compared to others. This is actually recommended because, for optimum profitability and performance at the market, a trader should use trading styles and strategies that they are most comfortable with.

There are plenty of strategies that can be used. They include intraday trades or day trading, long-term trades, scrapping, and swing trading among others. Of these, the most popular strategy has to be swing trading.

What is Swing Trading?

We can define swing trading as an approach whose main purpose is to gain and make profits in the course of a few days to a few weeks. It is a form of trading where traders endeavor to benefit from small market movements which can have a huge range in comparison. The average swing trading plan lasts between a single day and 5 days. However, it is common to see trade plans last a couple of weeks or even months.

Swing traders enjoy the potential of earning from breakouts within a relatively brief period of time. Part-time traders who have other things to do such as employment can benefit greatly from this method. It is easy to enter trades and then proceed to attend to other matters. Therefore, if you are a busy individual without the time and focus needed for short day-trades, then swing trading is probably the most appropriate strategy for you. Swing traders generally use technical analysis to guide them in their trades. Technical analysis involves studying a particular stock's history and using the information obtained to predict future movements. The reason is that past performance has been shown to be a great indicator of future price movements at the markets.

Technical Analysis

Technical analysis is very popular with swing traders. As such, they are least concerned about fundamental analysis and its implications. They do not care about a company's performance or its fundamentals. Whether a company is doing well or performing poorly is really none of their business. Even the thoughts of analysts, stockbrokers, finance experts, and others do not matter. The only important factor as far as day traders are concerned is the performance of the company's stock at the markets.

Swing traders often search for stocks with potential. Apparently not any stock traded at the markets qualifies to be traded. A good stock is one with a positive market outlook, one that has plenty of volatility, high volumes, and possibly a blue chip. Blue chips are valuable companies that are very successful and generate a lot of income.

The search, once relevant stocks are identified, focuses on positive risk versus reward ratios. Swing traders are aware that a suitable stock, once identified, is likely to make a move. It is crucial therefore to be there ready and waiting in order to capitalize on the movements. Swing traders need to be very fast and jump into a trade then begin to ride it.

Market Speculation

Swing trading can be viewed as a form of market speculation for the short term. In this fundamental type of speculation, traders hold positions for at least one day but usually for longer. There are numerous securities that can be traded this way including currencies, options, stocks, futures, cryptocurrencies, and even ETFs.

A trader will endeavor to make gains by entering a position and maintaining it for a day or longer in the hope of making some explosive gains. The time period ranges from one day to a couple of weeks. When this time period extends to months, then the trader is said to be an investor. The main distinction between traders and investors is the amount of time spent holding positions.

Trading the Downward Trend

Some traders prefer to enter a bullish market and apply swing trade strategies. Entry into such trade requires the use of a limit order, specifically the buy-stop order. Most traders prefer trading either stocks or options. Call options are preferred in a bearish market as traders profit under such market conditions. Options trading a bearish market can be rather complicated but it is an art practiced and favored by many seasoned traders.

Stocks and options on a bearish market tend to follow a zigzag or step-like path. In such a case, the stock will decline in value for a number of days, and then experience resurgence before resuming the downward trend again. With close observation and time, the overall trend can be viewed in much the same way as the upward trend.

Gains collected on the Downward Trend

First of all, you should only enter a bearish trade after carefully evaluating your risk versus reward ratio. We can compare the entry point, in this instance, with the stop-loss point. If the stock option or stocks attain the lowest price level of the most recent downward trend, then this point will be considered the take profit point so it is advisable to take profits and exit the trade.

Trading against the Markets

As a swing trader, you will mostly follow the trend set by stock on the market. Going with the trend is advisable and is what most traders do. You must be super talented or experienced to go against the trend. However, there are traders who do this. Such traders are said to be "fading".

Fading is simply another term for trading against the market trend. There are other terms used to mean the same thing. These include trading the fade, contrarian trading, and counter-trend trading. Sometimes, swing traders choose to trade the fade. This is where they assume a bearish position during an upward trend and a bullish position during a downward trend. As a trader, you want to exit any fading trades before the end of the counter-trends. This is because the trend will resume its normal movement and your positions could start making losses.

Swing Trading vs. Day Trading

Day trading is similar to swing trading in certain aspects. The major difference between the two is that trades entered in day trading are closed that very same day. Trades usually last only a couple of hours, and sometimes, even minutes. This is totally different from swing trading where trades can last for days, weeks, and sometimes, even longer.

Swing trading requires less time on the trading platforms compared to day trading. You do not need to sit down all day observing your screen and noting all the tiny movements that occur during the day. Day traders can hardly afford to leave the trading platform as they risk losing money.

As a swing trader, you are able to maximize profitability in the short-term by benefiting from most of the market swings. You can also rely solely on technical analysis to carry out trades and still be profitable.

The only major challenge when it comes to day trading is that you can be exposed to unexpected risks on the weekends or overnight. This is likely to happen when major events or announcements are made that can affect stock price movement. You can sometimes lose money on your trades when there is an abrupt or unexpected market reversal. And, sometimes, you may lose out big time on long-term opportunities by pursuing pretty short-term trends.

In essence, day trading and swing trading are very similar in some aspects. The major difference is the holding time. The minimum holding time with swing trading is overnight while day traders have to close out their trades before the expiry of the trading session. Positions are always limited to a day.

When a position is held overnight, certain things can happen. For instance, the trend could head downwards or the position could suffer risks like gaps. Both day and swing traders have access to trading margins from their brokers. A margin is simply a loan granted by the broker to clients for purposes of enhancing trades. Swing traders have access to about 50% leverage which means that a trader can receive a loan of up to 50% from the broker.

Preferred Day Trading Approach

Swing traders prefer dealing in multiple-day rather than single-day charts. Common chart patterns that are favored by swing traders include triangles, flags, head and shoulder patterns, cup and handle patterns as well as the moving average crossovers. However, each trader is expected to come up with their own trading strategy that suits their purpose, style, demeanor, and so on.

The best approach is to identify and come up with a strategy that provides one with an edge over numerous other trades. To come up with such a trade, a trader will need to identify suitable trade setups that point towards predictable movements of the chosen asset. Achieving such a feat is never easy and even the best strategies do fail some of the time.

No trader is victorious on each trade. Even the most successful and well-known traders such as Warren Buffet lose out one some trades. All you need is to identify a suitable and favorable risk versus reward ratio. In fact, to be profitable, you will only require a very favorable risk to reward ratio without the need to be successful in all your trades.

Foundations of Swing Trading

Swing trading has the potential to benefit from explosive price movements of stock within a pretty limited period of time. Most of the time, a trader will not be concerned about certain things. For instance, you will not need to concern yourself about a company's fundamentals, the kind of services or products they offer and even their trading name.

As a swing trader, you will be making your trading decisions depending on the demand and supply forces in the marketplace. There are two things that will concern you the most. For starters, is there any money headed towards the chosen stock or is it hemorrhaging funds? Even as you identify a preferred stock, you will need to find a way to enter trade while not exposing your trading capital to any unhinged risks.

A lot of traders like skipping the basics because they believe they have a good understand and foundation of trading. If you wish to be unsuccessful in your trades then you can skip this section. Otherwise, all successful traders take the time to learn and refresh their knowledge of swing trading fundamentals.

Perseverance

Novice traders are often excited at the prospect of swing trading. They are usually extremely eager to get started thinking about all the money out there waiting to be made. People are generally attracted to the markets because of the opportunity to make money on a regular basis.

At the onset, most traders believe that trading is easy and straightforward. Many get into the markets after reading a blog or book and getting inspired by the words they read. Often, there is a story about a successful individual who managed to hack the markets and earn a fortune. However, with time, some realize that things are not that easy or straightforward. Some will quit and only the most determined will remain.

Trading requires hard work and dedication. It also requires patience as well as experimenting with different styles until a trader identifies one that suits him the most. Take some time and do your research. Learn as much as you can about the markets. However, do not start searching for the easiest way out because nothing in life is easy.

Other important factors that affect the choice of a trading system include money management, risk control, and positive expectancy. When a trader is well aware of these crucial trading aspects, they begin to think about incorporating them into a strategy and trading system. With a good system and plan, a trader is able to fit in a trading plan that works for him or her in the long term. Get-rich-quick thoughts disappear pretty fast as reality hits home.

Chapter 1: Swing Trading Basics

Swing Trading is a momentary stock trading style. You take little benefits, cut misfortunes snappier, and hold stocks for less time. To make it work, your principles for trading should be specific to the shorter period. In spite of the fact that the additions may be littler, the shorter holding time frame implies you can intensify your increases into huge benefits after some time. Here are the essentials of executing a swing trading system.

Smaller Gains, Smaller Losses

As opposed to focusing on a 20% to 25% benefit for a large portion of your trades, a progressively humble 5% to 10% will be the primary benefit objective. The difference is to a great extent because of the holding time frame. Swing trades didn't take place months ago. It's increasingly similar to two or three weeks. By taking the little additions, frequently in transit up, you get most of a speedy move and evade the territories when the stock solidifies. Try not to anticipate selling at the top constantly. You'll regularly observe stocks go up more and kick yourself for selling too soon. Be that as it may, you'll additionally, in general, keep away from market amendments.

When you take benefits in transit up, if no new arrangements present themselves to supplant the sold stocks, you've normally diminished your introduction. Swing trading system put IBD's Swing Trader in real money right on time in the 2018 Q4 remedy and did likewise for the financial exchange revision in February and March of a year ago. You may finish up getting out too soon yet you can generally repurchase stocks if they recoup.

While you are taking benefits rapidly for most stocks, at times, you may have enough starting solidarity to warrant giving a stock more space to run. Because of an incredible hole up, Swing Trader neared its 10% benefit objective for Fibria Celulose (FBR) in only two or three days. We sold half and let the rest of for an increase of 20% in only 15 days.

Obviously, only one out of every odd stock thought will work. Slicing misfortunes rapidly is critical to keeping your portfolio sound. You can have just a large portion of your trades end positive and still make a great deal of cash as long as you keep your misfortunes little contrasted with your additions.

Swing Trading Example: Paylocity Stock

Specialized examination assumes a bigger job in a swing trading methodology, yet it's still a great practice to concentrate on organizations with excellent essentials. Take the Paylocity (PCTY) stock. It was under thought for Swing Trader with the ideal Composite Rating of 99. Yet, there must be some sort of revision that offers you the open door for purchase. In the case of purchasing a breakout through an opposition or an inversion, a redress goes before the buy.

> On May 9, Paylocity stock destroyed back to a purchase point around 91.70 and discovered help (1). The market activity on Swing Trader effectively turned wary the day preceding, going to sideways, as did the market standpoint in The Big Picture in its change to upswing under strain. The securities exchange declined on May 13 as the Nasdaq composite and S&P 500 cut through their 50-day moving normal lines. We exchanged Swing Trader market activity to a downtrend, and The Big Picture called the market in remedy. Strangely, Paylocity stock held over its past low on May 9, indicating relative quality (2).

That is the sort of specialized activity we search for notwithstanding the crucial quality. At only two or three weeks, it was unreasonably short for any of our customary base examples. In any case, for a swing trading methodology, the shorter holding time frame considers shorter unions.

> On May 16, the Nasdaq composite and S&P 500 got back over their 50-day moving normal lines. Our swing trading methodology was as yet careful of potential securities exchange headwinds. In any case, if the market bounces back proceeded, it could be useful for at any rate a transient swing trade. That day, the overwhelming trading volume went with a solid move in Paylocity stock as it cleared the 100 imprints (3). As the revision in Paylocity was gentle up until now, contrasted with the securities exchange, the relative quality line was at that point in the new high ground (3). By the nearby, we previously had a 3% benefit from our entrance on Swing Trader.

Sadly, the benefits didn't last. Market lists fell appropriate back beneath the 50-day moving normal line the following day, and we evacuated Paylocity stock right on time to secure benefit (4). Taking increases rapidly in an intense market is a colossal advantage of swing trading procedure. The market declined, and we evaded the trade turning negative on us and rather left with a 1.4% increase. That may not be a great figure but rather think about what it benefited from a solitary day in an extreme market.

Duplicate that regularly enough, and you'll have an incredible year as your increases compound.

How Swing Trades Works

Swing trading tries to exploit the upward and descending "swings" in the cost of security. Traders plan to catch little moves inside a bigger in general pattern. Swing traders expect to make a lot of little successes that mean significant returns. For instance, different traders may hold up five months to win a 25% benefit, while swing traders may acquire 5% increases week by week and surpass the other trader's additions over the long haul.

Most swing traders utilize day by day graphs (like an hour, 24 hours, 48 hours, and so on.) to pick the best passage or leave point. Be that as it may, some may utilize shorter time allotment graphs, for example, 4-hour or hourly outlines.

Swing Trades versus Day Trading

Swing trading and day trading seem comparable in certain regards. The fundamental factor separating the two procedures is the holding position time. While swing traders may hold stocks medium-term to a little while, day trades close inside minutes or before the end of the market.

Informal investors don't hold their positions medium-term. This regularly implies they abstain from exposing their situations to dangers coming about because of news declarations. Their increasingly continuous trading results in higher exchange costs, which can considerably diminish their benefits. They frequently trade with an influence so as to expand benefits from little value changes.

Swing traders are exposed to the unusualness of medium-term chances that may result in significant value developments. Swing traders can check their positions occasionally and make a move when basic focuses are come to. Not at all like day trading, swing trading does not require consistent checking, since the trades keep going for a few days or weeks.

Trading Strategies

Swing traders can utilize the accompanying systems to search for noteworthy trading openings:

#1 Fibonacci retracement

Traders can utilize a Fibonacci retracement marker to identify backing and obstruction levels. Given this pointer, they can discover showcase inversion openings. The Fibonacci retracement levels of 61.8%, 38.2%, and 23.6% are accepted to uncover conceivable inversion levels. A trader may enter a purchase trade when the cost is in a descending pattern and appears to discover support at the 61.8% retracement level from its past high.

#2 T-line trading

Traders utilize the T-line on a diagram to settle on a choice on the best time to enter or leave a trade. When security closes over the T-line, it means that the cost will keep on rising. When the security closes beneath the T-line, it means that the cost will keep on falling.

#3 Japanese candles

Most traders incline toward utilizing the Japanese candle graphs since they are clearer and decipher. Traders utilize specific candle examples to identify trading openings.

Having a steady and secure swing trading plan is a standout amongst the most significant traps of the market. Accomplishment in the business sectors is, to a great extent, a matter of order. It is tied in with having the ideal arrangement. A characterized swing trading plan goes about as a manual to keeping one on a trading way to thriving. Absence of arranging in cash the executives has its expenses and outcomes. Things being what they are, for what reason do you need a trading plan? All things considered; it is a significant formula for progress wherein you can have it both ways. Try not to depend on excelling in the business sectors, if you don't plan to be beneficial. Here is a portion of the top reasons why swing traders need a trading plan.

Swing trading plan

1. Apathetic Thinking= Trouble

To turn into a reliably benefit making trader, you have to get over apathetic reasoning, which causes the extinguishing of trading accounts. Self-control is the way to achievement in the business sectors, and a nitty-gritty Swing trading plan will keep you on the correct way.

2. Plan= Accountability

Having a well-characterized trading plan implies that one considers oneself responsible for specific norms. This is basic for improving responsibility as a trader and positively affecting swing trading. The swing trading plan fills in as a token of the best advantages for your trading account at some random point in time. Be that as it may, in the wake of investigating the business sectors does not help either. The more you dissed factors in the market, the greater test it will posture to your trading account. To understand your total potential as a swing trader in the market, persistence is the key.

Rehashing the blast bust cycle of the market will arrive you in money related doldrums. Continuing without an arrangement resembles monetary suicide. The best remedy for passionate trading missteps is a very much idea out swing trading plan.

This is on the grounds that the **arrangement depicts blueprints in a given market situation in solid terms. A brilliant trading plan shouldn't be excessively confused, yet it needs to be efficient.**

3. Trading= More Than Picking a Winning Number

Never liken trading with betting, on the grounds that the two are altogether different. It is critical to decide your entrance procedure. The passage point can have a significant effect between representing the moment of truth in trading. Regardless of whether you are reemerging toward a market pattern or setting off a moving normal, realize that arranging can assume a significant job in progress and disappointment.

4. Hazard Reward Analysis= Guarding Against Losses

The hazard to compensate situation on a potential trade set up before one enters it is a significant factor to consider. There ought to be lucidity in regards to the swing position estimating. Changing position measure while trading is basic for gathering the stop-misfortune separate. Going the other route round is essentially surrendering to voracity.

5. Exit Point= Clarity with respect to Strategy

One ought to be clear about the leave technique before entering the trade. This is the embodiment of fruitful trading. If you figure you will make sense of it as trading unfurls, be set up for stuns. When you are not in a trade, you are the target, and this is an ideal opportunity to set up your parameters.

6. Trading Plan=GPS for Trades

A trading plan has likewise been compared by specialists to a GPS gadget in that you enter where you need to proceed to check if the GPS has put you destined for success. Realizing when you've made an off-base turn, altering your developments with the goal that you can be pointed back the correct way.... these are a piece of having a trading plan.

A trading plan is much similar to a GPS in that it focuses you the correct way and causes you to accomplish steady benefit. It likewise encourages you to trade short your feelings and in addition to a ton of solace. Trading without much forethought includes depending on instinct and speculations, making it progressively about betting and less about managing in protections.

7. If You Fail to Plan, Then You've Already Planned to Fail

A trading plan is no certification of accomplishment. Be that as it may, a great trading plan will assist you with being a piece of the game longer than the individuals who don't have a trading plan. There are additionally numerous commonsense manners by which the trading plan will be useful to traders.

8. Great Trading Plan= Managing Risk Better

High or okay conveys unique importance. By putting a number to this, you can survey the precise degree to which this trade is hazardous. Hazard per trade scale could change contingent on your craving for taking risks and what you bring to the contributing table.

9. Setting up Strategies Beforehand= Less Stress, More Profits

Setting up section and leave methodologies in advance will lower pressure and make supports for making benefits. Enthusiastic reactions blemish chances at benefit; methodology stays at work past 40 hours. Build up certain section and leave criteria just as standards to stick to.

Graphs can be utilized to track market slants and considering passage or exit depends on target investigation instead of gut-level reasoning.

10. Savvy Trading Plan= Streamlined Decision Making

Money related markets move with stunning speed, and this is when trying not to be raced into ill-advised choices. Trading plans are a point of reference inside the circumstance fully expecting predicaments being confronted. Trading plans can remove the passionate remainder from the trading recipe. Already methodologies will survey the quality and rightness of your basic leadership process.

11. Trading Plan = Trading Diary

Think about your trading plan as a trading parcel or journal which you can use to follow every one of the trades and make notes concerning this achievement and disappointment. A trading log is a great instrument for taking a gander at the master plan, and you can get a fast perspective on the trading history and find slip-ups and blunders just as accomplishments in the bigger plan of things. For a depiction of the trading hits and misses, nothing beats a decent swing trading plan.

12. Proficient Trading Plan= Fewer Trading Mistakes

Trustworthiness and mindfulness are significant in the market. Consistent evaluation of hits and disappointments in the market will push you to reject slip-ups made in the past as well as embrace what works and simplify your trading choices.

13. Substantial Trading Plan= Maintaining Trading Discipline

A trading system can be a speedy token of the objectives and restrictions looked by a swing trader. The composed arrangement is useful for following your trading order and adhering to it will guarantee that there are no deviations of any sort.

14. Trading Plan= Every Good Swing Trader's Move

Who needs trading plans? Each great swing trader worth his time and energy do. From first time amateurs to prepared experts, trading plans are basic regardless of what sort of trades you need to climate. Profiting by a trading plan is choosing what is to your greatest advantage and doing it.

15. Trading Plan= Edge Over Other Traders

Without a decent trading arrangement, you are basically betting. It is essential to make a trading arrangement and stick to it else you will discover numerous diversions along the way. It is insightful to have an arrangement with the goal that you can become familiar with the required data about the market, getting data in regards to trading essentials and fundamental methodologies.

16. Successful Trading Plan= Knowledge of Results

A skillfully confined arrangement likewise gives a targeted criticism in regards to whether a specific technique for trading is working or not. You can likewise investigate why you're occupied with trading a specific stock and settling on educated choices as opposed to irregular ones.

If you need to push your very own pontoon as opposed to paddle haphazardly in the waters, trading plans are basic.

17. Complete Plan= Comprehensive Research

Settling on irregular choices implies you come up short on the explanation for what you are doing, and this can't work in the business sectors. You need an edge, and a well- characterized plan can give you simply that. Along these lines, before making a trade, you have to concoct a decent trading arrangement.

> When you know the greatest hazard, which can be taken per trade, you have to think of passage standards and specific value developments, diagram examples, insights and different pointers of the market's wellbeing at the season of diving in. Leave focuses incorporate value developments, diagram examples, pointers or inversions of the sign which prompted the passage. Different elements to consider are whether you will utilize trailing stops, participate in dynamic trade the board and diagram time period to which ways out would be connected. In this way, be clear about your purposes behind entering and leaving the swing market and have an arrangement for this with the goal that you don't become mixed up in the center!

How It Differs from Other Types of Trading and Where It Is Applied

Dynamic traders frequently bunch themselves into two camps: the informal investors and the swing traders. Both try to benefit from momentary stock developments (versus long haul ventures), however, which trading procedure is the better one? Here are the upsides and downsides of day trading as opposed to swing trading, and the real differences between the two.

Day trading, as the name proposes, includes making many trades in a solitary day, given specialized examination and advanced diagramming frameworks. The informal investor's goal is to bring home the bacon from trading stocks, wares, or monetary standards, by making little benefits on various trades and topping misfortunes on unrewarding trades. Informal investors regularly don't keep any positions or claim any protections medium-term.

Day trading includes a novel range of abilities that can be difficult to ace. Investopedia's Become a Day Trader course gives a top to the bottom outline of day trading, total with over five hours of on-request video. During the course, you will take in everything from request types to

specialized examination methods to expand your balanced hazard returns.

Day Trading

The greatest draw of day trading is the potential for stupendous benefits. Be that as it may, this may just be a plausibility for the uncommon person who has every one of the attributes, for example, definitiveness, order, and persistence, required to turn into a fruitful informal investor.

The U.S. Protections and Exchange Commission (SEC) calls attention to that "days traders regularly endure budgetary misfortunes in their first long stretches of trading, and numerous never graduate to benefit making status." While the SEC alerts that informal investors should just hazard cash they can stand to lose; actually numerous informal investors acquire gigantic misfortunes on obtained monies, either through margined trades or capital obtained from family or different sources. These misfortunes may diminish their day trading vocation as well as place them in significant obligation.

The informal investor works alone, free from the impulses of corporate fat cats. He can have an adaptable working timetable, get some much-needed rest whenever required, and work at his own pace, in contrast to somebody on the corporate treadmill.

Informal investors need to contend with high-recurrence traders, mutual funds, and other market experts who burn through millions to pick up trading favorable circumstances. In this condition, an informal investor has minimal decision however, to spend intensely on a trading stage, diagramming programming, cutting edge PCs, and so forth. Progressing costs incorporate expenses for getting live value statements and commission costs that can include on account of the volume of trades.

Long-lasting informal investors love the rush of setting their minds against the market and different experts throughout each and every day. The adrenaline surge from fast flame trading is something very few traders will admit to, yet it is a major factor in their choice to bring home the bacon from trading. It's suspicious these sorts of individuals would be substance going through their days selling gadgets or poring over numbers in an office desk area.

To truly make a go at it, a trader must stop his normal everyday employment and surrender his relentless regularly scheduled check. From that point on, the informal investor must depend totally without anyone else expertise and endeavors to create enough benefit to pay the bills and appreciate a not too bad lifestyle.

Day trading is upsetting a direct result of the need to watch different screens to spot trading openings, and after that demonstration rapidly to abuse them. This must be done for a long time, and the necessity for such a high level of center and focus can frequently prompt burnout.

For some occupations in the fund, having the correct degree from the correct college is essential only for a meeting. Day trading, conversely, does not require costly instruction from an Ivy League school. While there are no formal instructive necessities for turning into an informal investor, courses in the specialized investigation and mechanized trading might be exceptionally useful.

Swing Trading

Swing trading depends on identifying swings in stocks, products, and monetary forms that happen over a time of days. A swing trade may take a couple of days to half a month to work out. In contrast to an informal investor, a swing trader isn't probably going to make trading a full- time profession.

Anybody with learning and speculation capital can have a go at swing trading. As a result of the more drawn out time allotment (from days to weeks rather than minutes to hours), a swing trader shouldn't be stuck to his PC screen throughout the day. He can even keep up a different all- day work (as long as he isn't checking trading screens all the time at work).
Trades by and large need time to work out. Keeping a trade for an advantage open for a couple of days or weeks may result in higher benefits than trading all through similar security on numerous occasions multi-day.

Since swing trading normally includes positions held at any rate medium-term, edge necessities are higher. Most extreme influence is normally multiple times one's capital. Contrast this and day trading where edges are multiple times one's capital. The swing trader can set stop misfortunes. While there is a danger of a quit being executed at a negative value, it beats the consistent observing of every single vacant position that is an element of day trading.

Similarly, as with any style of trading, swing trading can likewise result in generous misfortunes. Since swing traders hold their situations for longer than informal investors, they additionally risk bigger misfortunes.

Since swing trading is only from time to time an all-day work, there is significantly less possibility of burnout because of stress. Swing traders typically have standard employment or another wellspring of salary from which they can balance or relieve trading misfortunes.

Swing trading should be possible with only one PC and ordinary trading instruments. It doesn't require the cutting- edge innovation of day trading.

Key Differences

Day trading and swing trading each have focal points and downsides. Neither one of the strategies is superior to the next, and traders ought to pick the methodology that works best for their aptitudes, inclinations, and lifestyle. Day trading is more qualified for people who are energetic about trading full time and have the three Ds: conclusiveness, control, and industriousness (requirements for effective day trading).

Day trading achievement likewise requires a propelled comprehension of specialized trading and diagramming. Since day trading is exceptional and distressing, traders ought to have the option to remain quiet and control their feelings enduring an onslaught. At last, day trading includes hazard—traders ought to be set up to once in a while leave with 100 percent misfortunes.

Swing trading, then again, does not require such an impressive arrangement of attributes. Since swing trading can be embraced by anybody with some speculation capital and does not require full-time consideration, it is a feasible alternative for traders who need to keep their all-day occupations, yet additionally, fiddle with the business sectors. Swing traders ought to likewise have the option to

apply a mix of major and specialized examination, instead of specialized investigation alone.

The Most Important Thing: The Price Action

Value activity for swing traders is the craft of seeing individual candles to decide the likely course of a stock - without utilizing any specialized markers.

Eventually, investigating value activity discloses to you who is responsible for a stock. It additionally reveals to you who is losing control: the purchasers or the vendors. When you can decide this, you can pinpoint inversions in stock and profit.

Become familiar with the value activity tips on this page, and I promise you that you will be a superior swing trader.

How about we start.

Tip #1. Identify backing and obstruction levels

This is an easy decision. Identifying backing and obstruction levels is one of the primary things you learn in the specialized investigation. It is the most significant part of diagram perusing. In any case, how many traders truly focus on it? Very few. Most are excessively bustling taking a gander at Stochastics, MACD, and other drivel.

A few traders feel that a help or obstruction level is a specific cost. Wrong. It's a territory on a stock diagram. Give me a chance to give you a model.

The zones that I have featured are the right help and obstruction levels. Frequently you will hear traders state something like this: "The help level for XYZ stock is

$28.76." This isn't right. It's a zone - not a specific cost.

Tip #2. Break down swing focuses

Swing focuses (some call them "turn focuses") are those territories on a stock outline where significant momentary inversions happen. Be that as it may, not all swing focuses are made equivalent. In actuality, your choice to purchase a pullback will rely on the earlier swing point.

In the first place, there isn't much space to work with! The separation between the pullback and the earlier high is excessively little. You need more space to run with the goal that you can, at any rate, get your stop to make back the initial investment.

The subsequent issue is this: The earlier high (yellow region) is made out of a bunch of candles. This is a solid obstruction territory! Along these lines, it will be extremely difficult for a stock to get through this region. Rather, hope to trade pullbacks where the earlier high is just made out of a couple of candles.

Tip #3. Search for a wide range of candles

Wide range candles mark significant changes in notion on each outline - in each time span. They mark significant defining moments and can regularly be utilized to identify inversions. This stock switched within earlier wide range candles. For what reason would a stock do this? Since the majority of the traders that passed up "the huge move" presently have another opportunity to get in. This purchasing weight causes inversion. Straightforward, huh?

Tip #4. Tight range candles lead to hazardous moves

Limited range candles can likewise disclose to you that an inversion is unavoidable. This low instability condition can prompt touchy moves.

Restricted range candles disclose to you that the past force has backed off. Purchasers and merchants are in balance, yet, in the long run, one of them will assume responsibility for the stock!

Tip #5. Discover rejected value levels

On candle outlines, lower or upper shadows on candles, as a rule, implies that there is a mallet candle design or a falling star candle design (if the shadow is long enough). Despite the name, these shadows mean a certain something: A value level has been rejected.

Envision what this sled flame resembled during the (prior day it turned into a mallet). It was extremely bearish! Be that as it may, sooner or later during the day, the bulls dismissed the lower value level. I can envision the bulls saying, "Hello, hold up an only a second. You bears have taken this excessively far. This stock is worth considerably more than the value that you moved it to."

What's more, the purchasing starts.

Tip #6. Become familiar with the half standard

How might you tell if a light is significant? Simple. Hope to perceive how far it has moved into the earlier days go. If it moves at any rate half into the earlier days run, then it is significant. What's more, it is particularly significant if it closes in any event half into the earlier days run. This generally appears on the stock outline as a piercing candle design or an immersing candle design.

The majority of the significant inversions in this stock happened simply after a flame moved at any rate half into the earlier days go (some moved substantially more than half).

This idea is powerful to the point that I am suspicious of purchasing any pullback except if it moves in any event half into the earlier days run.

Tip #7. The hole and trap value design

All holes are significant "tells" on any stock diagram. In any case, there is one sort of hole that is particularly significant when investigating value activity (and pinpointing inversions). This is known as a hole and trap. This is a stock that holes down at the open however then shuts the day over the opening cost.

You can likely observe what's going on here. The stock holes down at the open. Everybody thinks this stock is going to tank. Be that as it may, it doesn't! Purchasers come in and move this stock ideal back up. You can take a gander at one of these candles and nearly observe the majority of the confounded faces on other stock traders!

Tip #8. Measure the profundity of a swing

How far does a stock move into the earlier swing? More than midway or less? The response to these inquiries is significant in light of the fact that it can decide the future course of the stock. The value activity moved mostly down (bolt) into the earlier swing (spotted line). This is great. If it remembered more than that, you might need to scrutinize the legitimacy of the move. This is because a stock in a solid pattern ought not to backtrack more than most of the way into an earlier swing. It should experience purchasing weight sooner than the midway imprint. Also, common stocks will invert directly at the midway imprint.

Tip #9. Back to back up days and continuous down days

Stocks will invert bearing after back to back up days or down days. Thus, it pays to remember this when you are hoping to purchase or short a stock.

You ought to dependably hope to short a stock after back to back up days. Also, you should hope to purchase a stock-after back to back down days. This is illogical for new traders since they will in general partner a stock going down as "terrible" (which means sell) and stock going up as "great" (which means purchase). Truth be told, it is the exact inverse!

Area of cost in a pattern

You have heard the truism, "The pattern is your companion." I state, "The start of a pattern is your companion!" That is because the absolute best moves happen at the earliest reference point of a pattern...

This stock broke out (even line) from a twofold base (circumnavigated). Another pattern has started. Along these lines, you need to purchase this stock on the primary pullback (bolt) after the breakout.

Along these lines, there you have it. These value activity tips and traps will profit in the securities exchange.

You can utilize this data to make your own trading methodologies and frameworks. The best part is that once you ace this craftsmanship, you will never need to depend on specialized markers again to settle on trading choices.

They won't be fundamental.

Value activity portrays the attributes of security's value developments. This development is frequently broken down for value changes in the ongoing past. In basic terms,

value activity is a trading method that enables a trader to peruse the market and settle on emotional trading choices dependent on the ongoing and real value developments, instead of depending exclusively on specialized pointers.

Since it overlooks the basic examination factors and concentrates more on later and past value development, the value activity trading technique is subject to specialized investigation apparatuses.

[Many informal investors center around value activity trading methodologies to rapidly produce a benefit over a brief timeframe outline. For instance, they may search for a straightforward breakout from the session's high, go into a long position, and utilize exacting cash the board techniques to create a benefit. If you're keen on day trading, Investopedia's Become a Day Trader Course gives an exhaustive audit of the subject from an accomplished Wall Street trader. You'll learn demonstrated trading systems, hazard the executive's procedures, and substantially more in more than five hours of on-request video, activities, and intelligent substance.]

Chapter 2: Characteristics of A Swing Trader

Success in many opportunities given to any individual can only be achieved if that individual knows how to handle that opportunity well and turn it into something that will benefit him. Everybody has their own definition of success and everyone has their own way to reach it. But for those people who aimed high and work hard to reach what they want, they are the ones who can be truly called successful and become the role model, or even envy, for others.

Swing trading is one example of an opportunity that is given and open to anybody who wants to try it. Many people have become successful in trading stocks. Unfortunately, some were not. Those who fail sometimes have common thinking of getting rich quick just because they know that somebody has become successful. They didn't even realize that that certain successful individual didn't reach that level in just one night. Tears and sweat have been shed as well as late-night sleep just to be successful. That is the difference between the two. Working hard and being determined are just some of the traits that a successful trader possesses. There are still many traits that a person should have when they decide to start their journey to swing trading.

Below are some, but not limited to, characteristics of a successful trader:

- They should have self-discipline.

You should not be disciplined just because you need to be disciplined. You should possess self-discipline and apply it to every area of your life, not only in your career. People who have self-discipline know how to behave and react calmly to any situations. That is one thing that a successful swing trader should have because he or she will know what to do, when to go or stop, and how to react. Always remember that self-discipline should be applied all throughout and for a lifetime.

- They should learn from their losses.

Swing trading is also a risk, so everyone should expect that there will be times when they will win, and other times, they will lose. This is always a part of trading. So, whenever you experience loss, you should despair and lose faith. Instead, you should always learn from the mistakes you've made and the losses you acquired. It is wise that you do not make the same mistakes twice.

- They should be akin to learning.

Swing traders are always learning and they are always eager to learn. It is because, every day, the market keeps on changing. There will always be new strategies and tricks that spring up. There will be new methods to trade and new persons to look up to. Ensure that you are always looking up to new trends, updates, and news and learning new ways to move around the market.

- Be yourself

The way you trade represents your personality. That is why you should be trading personally and not just copying somebody else. They have their style they are comfortable with and you have your own. You just need to discover what that style will be and stick with it. You should be willing to take a risk and step out of your comfort zone and just let out your personality. If you don't trade with your true self, you will be unlikely to become successful.

- They should know how to make their own decisions.

One of the reasons why traders should learn as much as they can is because they need to know how to make their own decisions and stick with it. They should be aware of news and events that are happening that are related to trading. However, you shouldn't be swayed by it too much. You need to keep your emotions and facts straight and decide with a clear head so that you won't regret that decision in the end.

- A successful trader should know how to follow their own trading strategy.

Every trader should have their own plan in place when trading. They shouldn't copy the plans of other people because they have set those up to fit for those need. Everybody is different so our needs are different as well. Learn what needs to be learned and plan what needs to be planned.

- Avoid and prevent from overreacting. Always be proactive.

A successful trader never allows their emotions to sway their decisions and plans. They never get carried away and get too emotional whenever something doesn't happen the way they want it. They always keep calm and think logically before reacting to every situation. This is the biggest hurdle that many traders face. Getting your feelings under control is a must.

- Patience is the key. A successful trader always takes his time.

Beginner traders are always afraid that they will lose the profits that they have. That is the reason why they are quick to take those profits. However, that is one mistake that they should learn from. They must always keep in mind that wealth is accumulated slowly and cannot be acquired in just a night or week. A successful trader is always slow in making profits and quick in taking losses.

- Hide your ego.

This is not only applicable to trading but also to every part of our lives. A successful trader always has respect and stays humble. They are disciplined and not full of ego.

- They widen their scope of learning.

Traders that are successful don't just stick to one topic of learning. They also acquaint themselves with other knowledge that can be useful to their trading. They always branch out to other related areas and learn as much as they can.

- They always keep their trading records accurate.

Never, ever make trades and forget to record it. Trading records are really important not only to keep track of your trades, but it is also used for tax purposes. Also, you can always look back to your trading records and learn from the losses you have made in the past so you do not make the same mistakes.

- They also know how to live their lives.

Successful traders don't live their lives staring every day at their computers and monitoring the progress of the market. They also know that they only live once, hence, they know how to get out and enjoy their lives outside of trading. This is also their means to relax and unwind.

These are some personality traits that are needed by a beginner trader to become successful. They still need to learn more and hone their characters more to achieve the goals that they desire. Keep all of these in mind.

Chapter 3: Swing Trading Market Characteristics

The main goal of swing trading is to generate income. Each trader spends time on swing trading platforms with the aim of finding a stock whose prices are bound to move over a few days or weeks and make a profit from these movements. It is the responsibility of the trader to identify such stocks on the market using research and technical analysis methodologies. When used correctly, these methodologies increase your chances of making good profits.

How to Start Swing Trading

Swing trading is not very fashionable as found in stock markets today. It could be because it is an intermediate of day and long-term trading. If you are a beginner in this kind of trade, you may need to do a number of things to get started. We look at some of this below.

Identify a basic strategy. Swing trading is surrounded by several simple as well as complicated strategies. If you incorporate more advanced strategies too early in the trade, you may get frustrated and overwhelmed by the entire process. As you get into the trade, you must understand that it is not easy to master all the concepts at once. Starting out on complex patterns can make you miss vital parts of your trading positions and this will only mean one thing – loss of capital.

Have the market trend in mind. There are several swing trading indicators that you can use to determine the direction of the market. These enable you to predict future trends and use them to maximize your profits. In case the market has an uptrend, only take the signals going the same direction. The opposite is true for markets that are moving down.

Be patient. In every trade, there are profits and losses. In case you lose, do not get angry. Stick by plans, strategies, and tips that reduce the risk of losing your capital. This is because the market depends on several factors and in order to succeed in the trade you must incorporate most of these factors in your trade.

See the big picture. Swing trading involved a combination of several tools, charts, patterns, and pointers. None of these can work alone. Therefore, you should not focus on a single chart pattern, indicator or trend and believe that you will easily make a profit from it. Try out a combination of several of these.

Study stock patterns. As mentioned earlier, never get started until you have understood the direction that your ideal stock may assume in future. You can compare more than one trading instruments to establish any correlation between them. Avoid trading on stocks that are taking the same direction all the time since by doing this you will double your risk. There are particular types of stocks that perform better in swing trading than others. There are also times when some become too static or too volatile. You must have this in mind as you begin to trade.

Start with a demo account. If you are new to swing trading, it will be better if you make isolated trades first before increasing the number of positions you enter at one go. If you still have doubt about the platform you are using, start trading using a demo account just to get acquainted on the process and what is involved.

Trading costs. To get started, you only need a trading capital and transaction costs. For most platforms, you can easily start swing trading with as little as $5000.

In summary, swing trading basically involves getting the right market and the right stock. The best traders normally select stocks that have high fluctuation rates because these result in huge profits. As a beginner, however, you should focus on markets that possess less risk and shorter trading periods. As time goes by, you can increase the trading periods significantly since you will be able to manage the risks involved.

In case you need to make higher profits within a short period of time, you may consider trading in stocks that belong to large companies. These are often known as large-cap stocks and are always on high demand because of the high returns.

Swing Trading Terminology

Several terms are used in swing trading. As a trader, you must understand what each of these terms refers to for you to trade successfully. Let us look at some of the popular ones.

Bid: the best price or offer to purchase a certain stock or security

Candlestick: a charting method used by traders to predict price changes in a swing market. Candlestick patterns can also help you identify swing low and high points in trade charts.

Downtrend: A state when the price of a stock or security is on the decline.

EMA: This stands for the exponential moving average. It is one of the strategies used in swing trading.

Pullback or retrace: A non-dominant occurrence where the price of a stock moves in the same direction as the market trend.

SMA: An abbreviation of a simple moving average. This is also a strategy in swing trading.

Trendline: A line used to define the trend of a particular stock on the price chart.

Uptrend: A state where the price makes more highs than lows

Volume: Refers to the number of shares trader for each stock item over a period of time.

Swing trading is one of the techniques that allow you to hold onto a stock for some time before releasing it. The prices are often determined intra-weekly or intra-monthly.

The Swing Market and Large-Cap Stocks

Large-cap stocks are always on high demand when it comes to swing trading. Most of these stocks belong to fortune 500 companies that have a history of good prices and favorable trading terms. Swing traders take advantage of these stocks because they feature large price fluctuation ranges that translate to big profits. Since the changes in pricing occur within short time spans, traders make quick profits from this both in bullish and bearish markets.

Most companies that feature large stocks are also the best when it comes to chief exchanges.

Swing Trading Markets

Generally, swing trading operates in two market types: the bull market and the bear market. If you find yourself in between these two trades then you are at the right position to swing trade.

Swing trading works best in markets that begin well at position entry, decline for some time then rise again as the trading period ends. As a trader, you must understand which trades to make during bearish and bullish periods. An ideal swing trading environment is where market prices are not moving at all. During a bearish or bullish market, the momentum always carries stock in the same direction for a long period of time. Just like long-term trading, the success of swing trading is often based on how correct the trader identifies the current type of market.

Most markets change very little as time goes by. Some do change in a few days; decline for more days then rises again. Small swings happen more often than big ones. By the end of the trading period, the market would have made several upward and downward shifts. The main essence of swing trading is capturing some profits from these small yet frequent swings. Swing traders should select trades from stock that is active, and one that has a tendency to swing in well-defined patterns.

Counter Trending Swing Trading

Counter trending refers to the process of making a profit from the frequency at which swing trends break down. As noted earlier, each time you spot increased highs in a swing trading chart then there is likely going to be a continuous uptrend on the market. More decreasing lows signify a downtrend on the market.

Most markets start high and then are followed by retracement periods before stabilizing. A counter-trend seeks to make a profit from the retracement or reverse period. In this case, the trader monitors an uptrend pattern than when the line reaches a new high and starts to break; he buys stock in anticipation that the price will reverse direction.

When it comes to counter trending, the trader must maintain a high state of discipline so that the prices do not work against him. If the market assumes a trend that can make you lose, you must decide whether to exit the position or give it some more time. You must, however, bear in mind that if the trend does not break again you may lose a lot of money.

Swing Trading Systems and Software

This refers to programs that help you to leverage your trading strategies by making it easy for you to establish market trends and other important features. They identify trading opportunities on your behalf, saving you time and resources. Some of the best software programs make suggestions on the type of stocks that you need to trade in and alert you when to buy or sell at a profit.

Trading systems often take the form of charts. They help you to identify trends in the marketplaces and make winning trades. If you have been into swing trading for some time now, you agree that predicting stock prices manually from historical trends is not easy. This is where trading systems and programs come in. the systems utilize oscillations to obtain information on the stock prices. Traders who utilize such systems in their transactions can easily leverage on short-term stock price changes without fearing about competition from other investors.

Swing trading systems are not meant for everyone. They are mostly used by part-time traders who do not have enough time to enter market positions and monitor price changes all the time. Some of these traders only get to check the market once in a day or even week and therefore rely on information released by brokers. Expert traders can also use trading systems once in a while to make small profits.

One downside of these systems is that they only work in stable market environments. This is because such markets only make small changes in prices that can be easily ignored. However, a good system is capable to make good profits from these changes. The systems do not work well in bearish and bullish markets because the price only moves in one direction instead of fluctuating.

As a trader, you must, however, test any system to ascertain that it works before using it on your real trading account. Typically, swing trading markets change in four phases.

Phase one is where the market is bound by a certain range. The price oscillates between two boundaries and these are treated as the upper and lower boundary for the trade. Simple systems make money from this by initiating a long position at the upper boundary and a short position at the lower boundary.

Phase two is where the price goes beyond the upper boundary and stabilizes into a trend. The price then continues to rise and fall alternatively until the peak swing is reached. This results in another trading range and can be considered as phase 3.

During the last phase, the price drops from phase three and goes below the trend.

Most trading systems take this into account when creating positions. A good system is always capable of detecting whether the market is within a bound range or if it has started trending. Some systems work well when the market is trending but are useless when the range is bound. This is why you must test a system's feature before using it for your swing trades.

Swing Trading Plan

Just like a trading system, a system trading plan helps you manage your trades. Having well-defined objectives and possible outcomes of a trade are very essential when it comes to swing trading. A trading plan ensures that you remain consistent in your trading routine. It removes any guesswork that comes with not having a strategy. Discipline is what makes every successful trader.

A sound plan also helps you to analyze and adjust your trading history and strategy in a way that minimizes loss. Depending on the outcome of your trades, you can easily tell if your plan is effective or not. The plan keeps you away from outside interference as you set to understand the right times to trade.

One item that must appear in your plan is the study of swing charts. These are graphic figures that represent changes in the price movement of certain stocks. Swing charts are often easy to understand because they eliminate the noise found in bar charts. With swing charts, it is easy to identify features like:

- Support and resistance levels
- Swing highs and swing lows
- Chart patterns
- Channel areas

Stock strength

Traders can use each swing high and low on these charts as a trendline. Each chart features several meaningful points including flags, pennants, double tops, double bottoms among others. These are often straightforward in swing charts. It is also easier to apply tools such as trend lines, retracements and extensions on swing charts than it is for any other charts.

Trading Routines

Unlike other forms of trading, swing trading utilizes both technical and fundamental analysis to track price movements and establish momentum. Using this type of routine helps raise higher returns from a very small capital. The downside of this is that the process involves high commissions and volatility. In addition to plans and routines, swing traders must be willing to learn all the time. Most trading experts have an upper hand over starters because they are more experienced and enjoy lower commissions. They have enough information about the trade and make use of it to make consistent profits. Let us look at how a typical swing trading routine should look like.

Pre-market – most retail swing traders begin their day at 6:00 am or just before the opening bell sounds. The reason for starting early is to study the market and determine how the day is going to be. The first task should be catching up on the latest development and news on the market as these affect stock prices in some way. In terms of news, you should keep an eye on the following three items:

- The overall market sentiments including economic reports, inflation reports, currency performance and whether the market is bullish or bearish
- Industry or sector sentiments
- Current holdings in terms of the earnings, filings, etc.

Finding potential trades – From studying the markets, the trader should then identify potential trades for that day. On many occasions, swing traders get into the market by carrying out fundamental analysis then exit the market by the help of technical analysis. Fundamental catalysts comprise of special opportunities in the industry as well as some sector plays. Special opportunities are often highlighted in daily financial news and include factors such as mergers and acquisitions, bankruptcies, restructurings, and other related ones. Most of these opportunities represent the risk you may face during the day but also deliver great rewards if researched carefully.

Sector plays can be found on reputable websites that provide financial information. For instance, you can predict the trends in the energy sector by checking out popular energy news sites. Getting a watch list – next is to make a watch list for some of the promising stocks for that day. These should be stocks that seem to be in trade and also possess a good trend. These are always listed on your trading platform's dashboard with their various entry prices, stop-loss prices as well as target prices.

Assess existing positions – the final step involves reviewing any of your existing positions. Check the news and trends related to these positions to ensure that your capital remained intact throughout the night. You can obtain this news by simply typing the stock's symbol on a news portal such as Google or Yahoo News. If there is any viable information on these platforms then you should study it to find out if it will affect your current positions in any way.

Market Hours

Market hours refer to the time you spent watching the market and trading in the stock. Expert swing traders utilize level II quotes to determine which investors are buying and selling which items and at what prices. As soon as an ideal market has been identified and entered, the trader begins to analyze trends so as to define an exit point. This is always done using technical analysis techniques like Fibonacci extensions as well as common resistance and support levels.

Entering a trade-in swing trading is not a simple process. The timing depends on the activities of the day. However, the process of trading and exiting is often easier since most of the guidelines are pre-determined.

Very few traders make use of after-hours to place trades. This is because, at such times, the market is always illiquid and further spread. An important thing to do at this time is to evaluate the trade's performance. It is always recommended that traders record all the transactions they engage in not just for performance evaluation purposes but also for tax calculations. The performance evaluation process always entails scanning through a trade's activities and identifying areas that need improvement.

From this routine, you learn how important the pre-market routine is important for your trading success. It is at this time that most trading opportunities are identified and scheduled accordingly. Market hours should only be set aside for entering and exiting positions and not for planning. After hours, on the other hand, should be set aside for evaluation and taxation. Applying this routine to your trading plan can help improve your trading experience significantly. If you combine this with good trading resources and tools, you will easily make a good income from swing trading.

Without a good plan, software, and routine, swing trading can be a difficult trade to master. Regardless of the market or type of stock that your trade-in, you must create a plan and routine that minimizes the risks involved, and maximizes the reward. Swing trading is one of the techniques that stands out from the crowd. Although it is neither focused on long-term trading nor on day-trading, it can yield good returns if you take time and understand every underlying concept involved in the trade.

Chapter 4:
Finding a Suitable Market

However financial markets have very different behaviors, and some are more appropriate to swing trading than others. Therefore, in this chapter, we will look at some appropriate markets in which you can as a beginner start swing trading. No bias favors a particular market; we will leave that up to you. Instead, we will try to evaluate what are and are not feasible markets for you to enter based on your initial capital.

Selecting a Financial Instrument to trade

Selecting a market in which to trade will be the first big decision you will have to make as there are several different financial markets and what they call financial instruments to choose to trade in. For instance, you can trade in shares, currency, futures, options or even crypto-currencies to name just a few. Which one you choose will depend on your interest in that field and also largely by the capital you have to trade.

The good news is that there are lots of financial instruments you can swing trade with. And each one of them has its own pros and cons. Here are some financial instruments that are considered suitable for swing trading:

Exchange-Traded Funds (ETFs): You can trade ETFs just as you would trade a regular company's stock such as Facebook (FB) or Apple Inc. (AAPL). There are ETFs for just about everything; they will track indexes and bonds, futures, commodities, stock sectors, and currencies.

Individual stocks: Possibly the most popular instrument for swing trading is trading individual company shares. There are some advantages and disadvantages to trading individual stocks compared to trading ETFs. For example, taking a position with an individual stock exposes you to the possibility of 'single event risk.' What this means is that if you are holding a long position on a trending stock, you can be vulnerable to sudden bad news. For example, if bad news about a security breach breaks, say regarding Facebook or Google, the stock can suddenly fall. However, if you were swing trading on a sector like technology that bad news might take time to affect the market.

Some of the more popular coins include, but there are many more:

- Bitcoin
- Ethereum
- Bitcoin Cash
- Ripple

Bitcoin, in particular, hit a bubble around the end of 2017 which resulted in about 80% of its value being wiped out during the 2018 backlash. Consequently, the steep price reversal led to a loss of confidence in trading cryptocurrencies, so interest has dropped significantly. But Bitcoin, in particular, has always been of interest to swing traders due to its regular periods of high price volatility for seemingly no discernible reason. Where may that put many a beginner? There are also plenty seeking potentially huge profits. As a result, Bitcoin and the other cryptocurrencies still have the potential for high price movements for swing trading.

Options: Options and Futures are a more sophisticated instrument that can be used in hedge funds and hedging positions, but they are also good for swing trading. Trading options and using them in a variety of strategies requires additional education and experience that are not quite covered here, but as a swing trader you should be aware of their existence and consider using them as you increase your knowledge.

How much Capital will I need?

This is one of the most common questions beginners ask, but there is no real satisfactory answer as it depends. The reason it depends is that the market or financial instrument you decide to trade in will largely decide what is and isn't a viable starting capital account. For example, if we take a beginner with only $1,000 of capital which must be considered as being disposable income – only trade with what you are prepared to lose – then the only viable financial instrument to trade safely is currencies using the Forex market. We say 'safely' because to avoid the risk of ruin you must only risk 1% of your capital per trade – we will explain this in detail later. Therefore, you can only in this case risk $10 per trade. Now that might not sound too bad, but we have to take the commissions and transaction costs into play. We can demonstrate this through a few examples:

However, what is a feasible minimum capital account and what is recommended are two completely different things. For example, a capital fund of $2,000 is feasible for swing trading in shares, if the transaction rates are lower than some online broker's platform that operates with a minimum account of $1,000 and charges as little as $3.75 per transaction. However, entering the market with such small capital will restrict the number of trades that are available to you as ideally, you would want to trade the large Cap stock which is less vulnerable to market price manipulation by the market makers. Consequently, many experts recommend a starting capital account as an absolute minimum of $8,000 for trading shares.

Tools and Platforms, you will need

If you are seriously entering the market, then you should do it professionally. You should consider it the way you would any other business start-up venture. Therefore, you must have the capital, knowledge and the tools to do the job. The first thing you will need is an account with a licensed broker as they will do the trades on your behalf. They will also provide you with a way to make the trades typically through an online system. You should, however, shop about and try their online simulators to make sure you are comfortable with the system and the information that they give you. Fortunately, online brokers and stock trading platforms are in abundance, but your choice may be restricted by the country in which you are currently residing.

However, if you are just starting out and you do not have a trading account, then do a Google search to find a broker in your country that has good reviews.

When considering a broker look for the following things:

Account type – There are several types of accounts that are available to you as a swing trader. There will be an investment account. This style of account allows you to trade within the limits of cash deposited in the account. However, there is also an account called a Margin Account which allows you to use the money or stocks in your account as collateral so that you can borrow money from the broker. This facility of getting a loan from the broker will give you more trading power; however, you must be aware that you are now trading on borrowed money. This means you are taking on far more risk.

Transaction fees – The cost of executing a trade must be taken into account as the commission can vary greatly in price between brokers. However, for a swing trader that is just starting out the transaction fees are not quite so important. This is simply because as a beginner you should only be doing a very limited amount of small transactions a month. If not and you start out over trading then the brokers' transactions fee are likely to eat up the majority of your profit. The good news is that there are online brokers that charge as little as $3.75 per trade, but the bad news is that if you are working off a $1,000 account and sticking to the safe 1% rule, even that small commission will take most if not all of your profit.

Platforms and Tools – You want a trading system that you are comfortable with, but they vary a lot. Some online trading systems give you a lot of added features such as charts and research. Others, however, will give you the bare minimum. Also, the quality of advice and tools can vary across different brokerages. Indeed, it is not just across brokerages as some firms will offer different classes of service depending on how much you're willing to pay. Nonetheless, to start out you will want a reliable online system that provides real-time quotes as well as a straight forward ordering procedure. It is also important to have a reliable system that will execute your orders immediately and also confirm your trades. That is the minimum you should be looking for, but it would be nice to have real-time charts, technical analysis tools (moving averages, support/resistance, etc.). If you are going to pay a lot for the broker's services, then you should expect research reports and opinions as well as their analysts' ratings. Fortunately finding a broker and online services is not difficult as there are many free resources and online tools available. Listed below are several excellent resources.

Finviz (finviz.com)
ChartMill (chartmill.com)
StockCharts.com (stockcharts.com)
Estimize (estimize.com)
StockTwits (stocktwits.com)
CNBC (CNBC.com)

Yahoo Finance (finance.yahoo.com)

Starting out Paper Trading

Practicing and learning the art or science behind swing trading is incredibly important. After all, what makes you think as a novice that you can just enter the market and beat the odds. The harsh reality is that you will need to practice and then learn from your mistakes. It is those defeats and your subsequent analysis that will give you the skills which will enable you to survive let alone be successful. Even if you are a skilled trader in other instruments or a hugely successful day or position trader changing codes means learning new strategies and specialized tactics. Nonetheless, as competitive as the markets are, paper trading does give you a method to practice and develop your skills. This is why and how you should do it:

- Before you, as a beginner place a live trade, you should make sure to take the time to test the waters by first trying trading out on paper. The first step is to decide the amount you want to trade. This amount will be determined ultimately by your capital and your risk appetite. But in this
- example let us keep the figures easy to work with so let's say it is $10,000
- Then you go about selecting your stock after some level of fundamental analysis you have concluded

that certain stocks look to be on a promising trend wave and worth trading.

- Now what you have to do is to write on paper or notepad the current stock prices and the number of shares you want to buy with their current selling price.
- Then you must subtract the commission and transaction fees from that figure.
- Divide that trading figure by the actual share price, but remember to round down as you can't own a 1/3 or 1/2 of a share.
- Then sit back and ride the wave as you track your trades. You can easily do this by checking the closing stock price.

An example of Paper Trading To let you see how well it can work here is an example of paper trading a virtual portfolio.

In this scenario, you will start with say $20,000 and five preferred stocks. You have $4,000 per investment, but we must take commission and transaction fees into the equation, so we are less a $20 fee for buying and selling that's $9,980 apiece. Hence, we are likely to buy along with this type of pattern:

Stock A: Bought 100 shares at $20 for $2000

Stock B: Bought 150 shares at $30 for $4500

Stock C: Bought 100 shares at $50 for $5000

Stock D: Bought 100 shares at $60 for $6000

Stock E: Bought 200 shares at $12 for $2400

Now what you want to keep in mind here is that the original share price isn't as significant as the percentage of price movement, i.e., the gain or loss. For example, if Stock B goes up from $4 to $34 per share. You now have $5100 in this position a profit of 11%. But the notable thing is if Stock E also goes up from $4 to $16 per share? Well, then you'd be at $3,200 in this position at a profit of 13%.

This is the thing you must remember it isn't always just about the price it is about your current position – this is determined by both the price and how much stock you hold. Paper trading is educational and can be helpful in surfacing some strange trading anomalies as well as effectively designing your own swing-trading strategy. After all, it is far better to make your mistakes on paper exercises than lose your money trading real stocks. Of course, there is a downside. It is boring, and you don't get the positive feedback that a real trade gives you – a tangible loss or gain – but you must practice and learn the skills and develop those tactics and then see whether your skills and research return a profit. An alternative approach and one many younger people favor is to use a simulator or demo account to test your skills.

Practice trading with a Demo Account

Should you find that paper trading is a bit boring, then an alternative is to use a demo account. Most brokers will give you this facility as it is a simulator that you can practice on. By all accounts, demo accounts are more enticing than paper trading as the simulators give you immediate feedback as to how your trades are performing. But of course, there is always a conflict of interest – remember they are trying to sell you a service - and you may well find that you can do no wrong. Instead, you should try out as many as you can, and practice swing trading with a wide range of tactics. At the end of the day, demo accounts are a great way to gain trading experience without losing your money. They are important to swing traders as they allow you to try out and experiment with new strategies and tactics. They also help you build confidence – but be aware some are vanity orientated - while you learn the basics of market trading.

Demos - are they realistic?

The problem with simulators and demo market games is that they are often too one dimensional. They do not sufficiently give the experience of actually losing or winning and one of the problems is they often have little context as the data is historical. But in real life, the market is based on three emotions; Greed, Fear and Hope. With the latter being the deadliest. There is no way to simulate these emotions at the depth required to represent real trading whereby you could be fabulously wealthy or wiped out in a few seconds. Instead, the best that demo accounts can do is to simulate the real trading environment without the emotions. It is not the same psychologically. Indeed, physically trading with pretend money in many ways can make you learn bad habits. Nonetheless, it is an introduction to the sometimes-overwhelming experience of the financial market's mayhem. Therefore, realistic or not it is still a very good way to practice. There is, of course, a dilemma as most brokers provide you with these free to use demos or simulators. The problem is that they want you to play and to boost your confidence and get you to trade. After all, that's how they make their money. Hence be very wary of demos where you seem to do no wrong and especially those that reward a winning trade with a pop-up acclaiming you to be a top trader.

Discovery – There is a school of thought that every trader should find their niche market by testing their skills and knowledge against different financial instruments. The belief is that it will allow you to get a feel for the market that is best suited to your temperament as markets do behave differently. An example would be that trading stocks will be different to futures or commodities.

Gain experience – Practice your techniques and strategies on paper or a demo before you risk your own money. Whatever you do practice at least entering and exiting positions, plus applying stops and limits. Also, you may want to start experimenting with short selling, but most importantly you will gain an understanding of risk and capital margin requirements, as well as in tracking your profit and loss.

Charting – The most important aspect that a beginner to trading needs to learn is how to read a chart. Even if it is just simple pattern recognition, it is invaluable in making informed decisions. Therefore, you should spend time learning how to interpret price charts. What is more, you should also test your tactics and techniques against these charts to validate their effectiveness by testing the technical indicators to surface illusive patterns.

Evaluate past performance – Just about all worthy analysis is based on historical data. Machine Learning and A.I. feed almost exclusively on historical data. These clever algorithms analyze past performance data to find ways to find better solutions. They also are a good way to determine and then hone your strategy before you put your savings on the line.

Trading tools – There are a myriad of resources available to you such as the financial news, forums, and social media but how you interpret the information is the decisive factor. We all have free access to the same general information, but some make it work for them while others let it drift by. Understanding how world events can affect stocks particularly within a sector is hugely important, so pay attention to news feeds and breaking market data.

Watch-lists – As part of your overall strategy have a list of potential stock that you would like to keep an eye on. These may be stocks that you aren't sure about, but you still should keep them in mind. Many experienced traders' regrets are over missed opportunities rather than bad trades so keep track of those borderline stocks.

Manage Risk – A demo account is hugely beneficial as you are betting with virtual money. Therefore, gains and losses are meaningless in real terms, but they should be tactically analyzed to prevent you from repeating the mistake with your own money. Also, demos allow you to practice swing trading so that you make your early learning mistakes in a safe environment and not in the big bad world.

Price action – Demos can give you plenty of practice in reading price lines and identifying trends. One of the best ways to interpret a price line is to spot the visual patterns; however, that only comes with experience. Practicing on real price lines on a demo will give you plenty of practice interpreting those volatile movements that will allow you to profit on future real price fluctuations.

Broker and platform – Trying out a broker's online platform is a good way to evaluate their service. You can, for example, see what research and charts they provide and also see what they charge extra for. Also, you can get a taste of how good they are by dipping into their forum and taking account of the sentiments of the regular poster.

Chapter 5: Tools for Every Beginner

When I discuss tools of swing trading, I am talking about all of the charts, equipment, and documents you will use as a swing trader. Some of these tools are already set up for you and you just need to learn how to use them. Other tools you will research and establish yourself, such as your generalized trading plan. Each tool is essential to reach success as a swing trader.

The Basic Tools

The basic tools are the tools you need to help you understand swing trading. Many people don't think about these as tools, but many are considered a factor when it comes to learning about swing trading.

Research Material

You may not realize this, but reading this book to help you understand swing trading is using a tool. One of the first tools you want to pick up when you start thinking about becoming a swing trader, whether part-time or full-time, is research. You want to read books that will help you understand the basics of swing trading. The key is to sit down and take on your first trade with the confidence of an expert. You want to feel that you will become successful because you know as much as possible about swing trading. Of course, you will still learn about the business along the way, but your confidence is essential and will build the more you read about swing trading.

Devices

Making sure you have a computer is a given. However, many experts will tell you that you want to invest in a desktop over a laptop. While a laptop is great, and you probably already have one, a desktop is more secure for trading, especially when it comes to the platforms you will use. Furthermore, you can't move around a desktop easily, meaning it will need to stay in one location. This is perfect for people working from home because they will focus more when they are in their created office space. This can limit distractions. It is always important to limit distractions when you work from home, but this is more important as a trader. When you are distracted, such as thinking you can watch your favorite holiday movie and focus on your research and trades at the same time, you are more likely to make mistakes and take a loss.

You also need to ensure that your computer is up-to-date. Get the latest software package, as most platforms need this to function correctly. You also want to invest in a good printer and any other software device that allows you to connect to your investments, such as an iPhone and tablet. However, you also need to keep distractions in mind and consider if you want to allow yourself the ability to work away from your desk. When it comes to the psychology of swing trading, it is best to separate your personal and work life as much as possible. Therefore, you don't want to allow yourself to have access to your portfolio or any of your work on your phone or tablet.

Financial Instruments

Another tool is the financial instruments you will use. These are stocks, cryptocurrencies, currency, exchange-traded funds (ETFs), and options. While I will discuss financial instruments in-depth later, they are an important tool to mention. Most experts believe a beginner should start with individual stocks, as they will give you the best foundation when it comes to trading. But you can also focus on ETFs, which is a group of stocks. You treat ETFs similar to an individual stock, but you are supporting a large number of companies within the stock. For example, one ETF can have about 100 companies, each with a small share within the ETF.

Even if you think you should start with stocks, look at all of the financial instruments available to you to get an idea of what each instrument is about. A little research will help you establish trading goals, as you might feel your best trading skills are with currencies, but you don't want to start with them immediately. Instead, you will look at starting with individual stocks and move toward currencies.

Trading Account

As a beginner, it is best you work with a broker. They will help you throughout the process, including watching your investments and making any trades you feel are best. One of the steps a broker will help you with is setting up a trading account. For instance, they will help you decide on a margin account or investment account. They will run through the account with you, so you can easily find anything you want at any time.

Trading Platform

If you use a broker, they will have a specific trading platform they use. You should do extensive research on brokers, their fees, and the types of platforms they use. There are several platforms and you might find one more suitable for you. For example, some platforms allow you to take part in real-time charting and provide analysts' ratings. Some will provide more research reports than other platforms. There are some platforms that are better for technical analysis and others that focus more on fundamental analysis.

Swing Trading Tips

One of the best tools you can receive as a beginner are tips. However, to take advantage of these tips, you need to remain mindful as a trader. This means you need to pay close attention to every detail within your trading career. Don't make a decision without fully thinking it through. Note every step you take and don't allow yourself to multitask when you are swing trading. Mindful means you are living in the present moment. You aren't letting your mind think about anything but your task. This means if you are researching, you are focused on what you are reading and not on your grocery list or what movie you want to watch that night. Keeping notes or highlighting important information will help you remain mindful.

Research Everyday

Some people think they will research the stock market before they start their new career and then stop focusing on the research when they feel like they understand the stock market, trading, and are generating an income. This is not the idea you want. Trading means you will research every day. In fact, you will spend most of your day researching companies, analyzing charts, and making notes to give you the best outcome. The more you research, the stronger a trader you will become.

Of course, this also means that you will start researching swing trading before you fully decide to become a swing trader. You might be in the "this might be the direction I want to go" mindset when you start researching. By the time you have completed a few Google searches, read books about swing trading, and possibly joined some forums and spoke with a few swing traders, you will have your decision.

Take your time when you research. There is never a step you want to handle quickly as a swing trader, even if you aren't sure you want to follow this direction. Many people suggest that traders start a notebook from the moment they decide to take on the career. You can use this notebook as a journal, allowing you to write down your notes and thoughts as you go through this process. Write down all the important information you believe you need to know.

Once you start trading, you want to keep your research to the historical charts of the company and stock you are thinking about trading. Analyze as many charts as necessary, whether these are daily, weekly, monthly, or yearly charts. Once you feel like you know the company and the direction they are going like the back of your hand, you are ready to create your trading plan and take on the investment.

Control Your Emotions

One of the hardest factors to follow as a trader is keeping your emotions out of your trades. Some people find it useful to use strategies to help them control their emotions. For example, they will meditate every morning or focus on deep breathing exercises when they become anxious about how a trade is going. This allows them to remain calm so they can make the best decisions about their trades. Your risk of making a mistake and taking a loss on a trade is high when you let your emotions take control and make decisions for you. For example, one of the reasons the 1929 stock market crash occurred was because people allowed their emotions to take over. While the economy and the stock market were on a downward spiral, the bottom line of the crash happened when everyone started to sell their stocks because they became worried about the stock market dropping more than usual. The way the stock market works depends on how many people are buying vs selling. When people buy stocks at an increasing rate, the prices of stocks will increase. This puts the stock market in a positive light. When people are selling their investments, the prices drop and other people won't purchase the stocks. If the market gets too low, it will crash. In other words, when you are watching a movie about traders on Wall Street and they yell, "buy, buy, buy!" or "sell, sell, sell!" they are allowing their emotions to control their decisions.

Many traders feel that they are "losing their mind" when they lose control of their emotions. On one side, they do not understand why they feel so strongly about a loss. On the other side, they continue to focus on the loss and many enter the five stages of grief. Even though some people feel it is overdramatic to go through these stages for a loss, it is common for traders at all levels. The main reason behind it is psychology. Suffering a loss of any type can place you on the path of grief.

The five stages of grief include:

1. *Denial.* When a swing trader reaches this stage, they can't believe that they are facing a loss. They were sure that this stock would improve their winning streak. Traders who are in denial will continue to think "it will turn around" instead of facing the fact that they are about to lose a lot of money.

2. *Anger.* The anger can show up as a disappointment in themselves or in the stock market. This is the stage where traders often talk negatively about themselves. Other traders start to believe that the stock market is against them and they should rethink their career. Another way trader handle their anger is to find someone else to blame.

3. *Bargaining.* No one wants to lose a lot of money. When traders see they are losing money, they will start bargaining. They might try to bargain with the stock market itself or God. They will do anything to

try to find a way out of the situation and not lose their money.

4. *Depression.* This is a dangerous stage of grief and one that traders feel strongly. Traders realize that they lost their money and they cannot receive it back. They will start to think about the mistake they made and wonder why they were not more careful. They become overly critical of themselves, and this tends to send people into a deeper depression. The way you handle this stage will set the tone for the next stage and when you enter it. At this point, it is important to mention that some people can enter a state of clinical depression. This is a psychological disorder that can last for months to years. In fact, many people battle depression their whole lives. While this is rare because of a trading incident, it can tip off the depression you already had. It is also different from the sadness you might feel after your realization of loss. If you are safe for a few hours to a few days, it is something you will move on from. If you find yourself depressed and uninterested in taking part in tasks you used to enjoy, you have a form of depression and you should look into counseling for help.

5. *Acceptance.* The final stage is acceptance. This is when the trader may still feel a bit of guilt and

sadness over their loss, but they have come to accept it and are working on moving on. They will often close out their trade at this point, mark it in their journal, and analyze their situation to see how they can avoid this happening in the future.

Treat Swing Trading Like Your Career

You need to take swing trading seriously. It doesn't matter if you decide to become a part-time or full-time swing trader, you have to treat trading like any other career. This means you will set your schedule and stick to it. You will limit distractions, so you don't find yourself making decisions while watching television or hanging out at the beach. You will do what you can to strengthen your self-discipline. When you establish guidelines and rules for yourself, you will follow through with them.

Another way to treat swing trading like a career is to set up a contract with yourself or create forms you need to sign, like any other job has their employees do. This can give you the added benefit of making your new trading career feel like a job, even if you are at home. If you have never worked at home before, you might find yourself struggling to keep your mind on track. It will help you by focusing on trading as your new career.

Join an Online Community

Many beginners don't think of joining an online swing trading or stock market community that can help them develop their new career. There are dozens of online communities that you need to consider joining. You don't need to join all of them, but you should join a couple that will give you the benefits you need. For example, you can get to know other swing traders with different experience levels, backgrounds, and tips. All of these factors can help you develop as a swing trader. Some of the best online communities to look into are Elite Swing Trading and the Trading Heroes Blog. These community forums will keep everyone up-to-date on your companies, major news that can affect your stocks, and other information.

You Will Make Mistakes

No matter how well you do as a swing trader, you will make mistakes. Instead of worrying about your mistakes, you need to learn from them and move on. Don't allow yourself to focus on the mistake, as this can influence any future decisions. Keeping your mistakes in your mind will also bring your emotions into trading.

One way to look at mistakes is that they are a part of learning. They will help you grow and become the best swing trader possible, as long as you use them as a tool for learning.

One of the biggest reasons you want a good frame of mind with mistakes is because they can cause you to lose sight of your mindset. When you focus on the mistake you made, you bring yourself down. You might ask yourself, "Why did I make such a stupid mistake?" or "Why wasn't I more careful?" These thoughts will lower your self-esteem over time. You need good self-esteem to stay in the winning mindset and become a successful trader. Instead of the negative questions to ask yourself you need to focus on more positive questions such as, "What can I learn from this mistake?"

Don't Ignore the News

Everyone does this from time to time. Some people don't like to read the news because they feel it's all "bad news." People want to read and hear about the good news happening in the world. While this is understandable, you can't let it take away from the news you need to read and know about as a swing trader. If you hold a stock for a company or are thinking about purchasing a stock, you need to keep the company in mind. Always look for news about your company, as most of the news will affect the price of stocks and your profit.

You can always receive notifications from Google about your stock's companies or look into Yahoo finance. There are several news media outlets that have pages dedicated to the stock market.

Find the Best Broker for You

Finding a broker is a step I will cover later, but it is extremely important you focus on finding the right broker. Don't settle for the broker closest to you. Instead, complete a Google search, look at the phone books (yes, they still exist), and do some research on your potential broker. You can look into their background through the firm they work at or by reaching out to your county's financial services. You want to make sure that your broker is trustworthy and you respect them. Furthermore, they need to have a clear understanding of swing trading. You also want to pay attention to any fees and commission costs of your broker.

Keep A Journal

Keeping a journal is not high on everyone's list. In fact, there are a lot of people who groan at the thought of keeping a journal. But once you start you will find the many benefits of keeping a trading journal and become attached to your journal. Not only does your journal help you stay organized, but you can also look back at your growth. You can analyze your decisions and see if there is something distracting you or if you are in need of guidance over swing trading. Your journal can help you keep track of your charts and any important information you find in your research.

To give you an idea of how a journal can help with swing trading, let's take a look at the following example:

Prince is in his second year of working full-time as a swing trader. He's done well for himself and does his best to maintain the winning attitude, learn from his mistakes, and control his emotions. He gets up at 5:00 a.m. every morning to make sure he can get ready for the day, have breakfast, read the news and get to his desk by 7:30 a.m. for the opening of the stock market. Over the last couple of months, Prince has found himself in a slump. While he continues to meditate every morning and focus on his successful trades, he is losing more trades than he did as a beginner. This is causing Prince to struggle with his mindset and question his abilities as a swing trader.

To find out what changed, Prince decides to go through his journal. About three months back, he starts to notice that he quit walking every morning. This happened because he got sick with a cold and didn't have the energy to walk. Unfortunately, though he wanted to, Prince never got back into walking. He also noted that he doesn't focus as much attention on the news. He used to spend about 45 minutes catching up on the news and now only takes about 20 minutes. Therefore, Prince decides to focus his attention on walking every morning and paying more attention to the news.

Over time, Prince notices his mindset change. He starts to believe in his capabilities and has more successful trades. If he hadn't written all his information in his journal, Prince would have never found out the reason for his slow decline.

Stay in The Winning Mindset

As you know, the winning mindset is important for a swing trader. This is the mindset that any trader needs to focus on, but it is more important for a swing trader. While I will focus more on what the winning mindset is, how to gain, and how to keep it, one of the strongest tips experienced traders give is telling beginners to stay in the winning mindset. This is not hard to do. It's a positive mindset and some people struggle to remain calm and optimistic. However, it is essential that you do this so you can reach the success you dream of as a swing trader.

The basis of the winning mindset is your confidence. You need to believe in your abilities as a swing trader. Another important characteristic is patience. You need to wait for the right moment to enter and exit a trade. Another important point is keeping your expectations realistic.

Chapter 6: Fundamental Analysis

Fundamental analysis is a process of looking at a business at the most fundamental or basic level. Think about it this way. If your cousin came to you and said they had started a business and wanted you to invest, how would you make your investment decision? Character issues of your cousin aside, you'd want to know what products and services the company was offering, and then you'd want to dive into the company's financial data to see what it's revenue, growth, expenses, and debts are. You'd also evaluate the company for its future potential.

When it comes to companies on the stock market, this is all that fundamental analysis really is. You're going to be doing the same procedure on a large publicly traded company. This may even include personality evaluations. If your cousin is crazy, you might be tempted by the business idea, but hold off on investing because you feel that your cousin would not be a good business manager. With publicly traded companies, investors might do the same if they don't like the board or management team, or just the CEO.

One of the debates among swing traders is whether or not they should use fundamental analysis or not. The truth is, that depends on the time horizons that you use in your trading. Since there are many different trading styles in swing trading, not all swing traders are going to be using fundamental analysis. However, fundamental analysis can be used by swing traders. If you are going to be holding your positions for weeks or months at a time, then doing a bit of fundamental analysis is going to be helpful in producing winning trades.

Even short-term traders should be doing some fundamental analysis. Do you have to dig into it to the degree that a Warren Buffet would? Of course, not – however, knowing what the company is up to and its financial health can help you choose better trades.

Swing trading generally doesn't require in-depth fundamental analysis. Unlike a long-term investor, you are not tying yourself to the company. However, you may want to do fundamental analysis in order to get a solid handle on the company's fortunes, especially on a quarter-to-quarter basis. Remember that a company that is solid when it comes to fundamental analysis is going to be attracting a lot of investment, including big investment houses. As a swing trader, you can take advantage of this as well, because that can push up stock prices.

One way that you can use fundamental analysis is to find companies that are going to be undergoing a long trend. If a company is posting solid numbers, it might have an ongoing uptrend in share price that can last weeks, a quarter, or even up to a year or more. Using the trade with the trend philosophy, these kinds of steadily rising stocks can provide profit opportunities for swing traders that are patient enough to wait out longer trades.

Earnings calls are generally to be avoided, in my opinion, but some do find opportunity there. These often result in major price swings. The problem with them is that before the fact, people are speculating without any real data to back up their beliefs. That makes getting in on a trade before an earning call a difficult proposition. One way to get around it is to hedge your bet. Hence, if the speculation is that a company is going to be reporting a good earnings call that is going to result in a large increase in share price, you can buy a lot of shares—but hedge your bet by also shorting the stock with a smaller bet so that you can cap your losses if there is a downturn instead.

There is the option of waiting until after the earnings call to make a move on the stock. This can work, but you need to be aware that there are many difficulties. The first is that you are going to have a very hard time getting in on a trade at the opening bell under these circumstances. The price of a stock can be rising or falling very fast if expectations are "exceeded," so fast that it might be hard for individual traders to execute a trade. You might have to place a limit order offering a higher price than you would really like to pay for the stock.

A second problem that sometimes arises in these situations is that in many cases, the rise or fall that is going to happen with a stock happens extremely quickly, and then after that, there is a long consolidation period. So, you might miss the boat entirely, and sometimes the boat leaves the harbor in after-hours trading.

Since this is a book about swing trading, we are not going to cover fundamental analysis in detail, but we will give readers an overview of how they can use some level of fundamental analysis in their evaluations of companies that are good to trade.

Earnings and Cash Flow

The first thing you are going to want to look at for a company is the state of its cash flow. You are not going to be looking into investing in companies for the long-term as a swing trader, so you are not interested in the long-term financial health of the company, per se. But remember that many other investors are interested in such things. So, a company with good cash flow, in particular, good net income that is increasing YOY, is going to be a company that is attracting a lot of investors. That, in turn, means that the company is going to be one that sees the stock prices pushed up.

Earnings are the most important factor with any company, but you need to look at some specific measures. One of these is earnings per share. This gives you the amount of profit the company is making per share, and this is something that can be compared from stock to stock. Keep in mind that you will want to compare apples to apples, so if you are looking at EPS, be sure to make comparisons between companies that are in similar sectors.

The price to earnings ratio is another important measure. This will help you determine if a stock is over or underpriced, given the fundamentals of the company. A company with a certain level of profitability that has a low P/E ratio is a stock that can be expected to rise at some point. These are the kinds of companies that a Warren Buffet may target, but you can target them also. Again, compare P/E ratios in a given sector. A technology company, for example, can be expected to have a high P/E ratio.

PEG or projected earnings growth is an estimate of the future growth rate of the stock. If this is a good number, this can indicate that this could be a stock you can profit from using a 90- to 180-day swing trade.

Price to book ratio helps you gauge the real value of the company. "Book value" is the value of the company on the books. You don't have to be an accountant to use it, most stock market sites publish the calculated values, and you can compare to like companies. If it is low, this could be a company that may enter an uptrend.

Other Factors

You will also want to take a look at the company's balance sheets and income statements. In particular, you want to see two things, in my opinion. The first is how much debt the company is taking on. Take a look at this, especially if the company pays dividends. If a company is taking on a large amount of debt, it is going to have less ability to pay dividends in the coming months. Dividends are a factor in attracting many investors, and if a company that pays dividends goes into a lot of debt, investors may end up dumping the stock. Just something to be aware of.

One situation to key in on is a company that had good revenue but a bad earnings report because of rising expenses. This often happens because the company has made investments that are going to improve its performance in the future. Thus, the one-time investments may reduce profits in the current quarter, but over the coming 90 to 180 days, the company is going to see improved profitability—and hence much higher stock prices—due to the fact that they won't have to make the investments again (at least, not in the short term) and that actual profits will grow. Thus, keep your eye on companies that are known to be profitable that might have a disappointing earnings report. Do the research to find out why, and if a company had bad earnings because it is devoting funds to investments for the future, it could be a good trade.

Chapter 7: The Psychology of a Successful Swing Trader

Simplicity Always Beats Complexity

One thing you should note about the investment industry is the fact that it is filled with complex terminologies and very busy charts. What is unfortunate is that most beginner traders confuse complexity as a requirement for one to succeed in the market.

Well, the truth is, you don't need any complexity in trading. There is no need for complex charts, data or even indicators for you to make a good trading decision of investment. It is often easy to get caught up in intellectual pursuits that we allow that to completely override our money-making efforts.

It is important that you stay simple when trading. Don't let being right or the desire to get great calls override the real reason why you are in the market. Being successful in trading does not mean complex screens, methods and tools, several technical indicators, or days staring at the screens.

What you need is the ability to adjust your opinion, have the fortitude to accept when you are wrong, get quality information, and have the ability to find confluences of support, resistance and unique thoughts about them.

How to Systematize Success: Plan–Do–Check–Act

When you are trading, one most important thing is to ensure that you have a trading plan.

Plan: what you need to do is plan a change and then test it. the main aim is to determine whether there is need for modification of the process for things to be more beneficial.

Do: the next thing is for you to implement that change and then try to test it on a small scale to ascertain the outcome.

Check: once you test the change, the results you obtain are relevant in determining what the important lessons are. Here, it is critical to note what went right, wrong and whether the changed worked out well or not. You can know how the change impacted the process by reviewing a 30,000-foot-level control chart and carrying out hypothesis tests.

Act: finally, it is important to note whether you would like to adopt the change, abandon it or redo the whole PDCA cycle. When you do not get any significant value from the process as you had initially anticipated, then it is safe to terminate the decision. If the change is expected to create adherence issues or bring about minimal improvements, then it is safe to abort or repeat the cycle. In other words, you are repeating the process because the amount of improvement is not as much as you had anticipated. However, you might have already identified opportunities for change enhancement.

Once your main objective is met, then the final thing is for you to standardize the whole process. The power of this process lies in its simplicity and inductive use of logic. While it is also easy to understand, it can be challenging to attain on an ongoing basis mainly because of difficulty associated with analytical judgment of the hypothesis.

Plan: Setting your goals, targets and strategies

When you start trading, there are so many questions you need to ask. Truth is, with all the information out there, it can be challenging to decide where to begin. However, you should set goals, targets and strategize but chances are that most goals traders make are the wrong kind.

The goals that you set in the beginning will help determine whether you are going to make money or lose money. Therefore, it is important that you make your goals about the process and emulating all the traits professional traders portray.

The first one is by ensuring that you have a plan. In business school, we are taught to start any business with a business plan. If you didn't know, trading is a business! This means that each time you trade, you have to trade according to a well-thought-out, and calculated plan.

Your trading plan should tell you how to enter trades and exit trades. It should include ways you intend to manage money. In other words, the whole plan should be well-detailed with risk parameters to look out for, markets to be traded, position size, whether you intend to use filters as trade signals, the market environments to trade and how you intend to determine such things as trends and ranges among others.

In short, your goal should be to come up with a plan before you trade.

Do: Setting up your trading routine

When a certain dollar amount is your goal, you will ensure that you push to achieve that goal irrespective of opportunities being present or not. The truth is, the market does not present statistical probability of trading opportunities always. In fact, you will be better off sitting on your hands in most instances.

However, this does not really work well for most people. Most people are looking to continually do something. The thing is, in the market this can be slow and risks eroding your profits during good trading times.

Understand that trading when the times are slow or when you make impulsive trades that are out of scope requires your immediate attention. Therefore, one of your goals should be to be disciplined as much as possible so that you only trade as outlined on your plan.

Check and act

One thing that you need to note is that a complex strategy can be quite alluring. So many people think that just because something is complex it is highly likely to work. You need to avoid being fancy with your analysis and trading strategies. Don't make your winning plan complex.

What you need to do is check the plan you have that it is realistic and simple, and then act on it. If you fail to check and act, chances are that you will destroy the profitability of it. If you truly like the stock market, then ensure that you stick to trading stocks.

The bottom line here is for you to ensure that you are not constantly tinkering. This way, your performance will improve. Instead of always trying to switch the market, analysis method or the strategy, simply stick to your plan, check through it and action. However, if you feel the need to rework it occasionally, ensure that you keep all revisions simple so that you don't end up making things overly complex.

How to set up a trade journal

When trading, one of the most impactful and highly leveraged activities traders adopt is keeping track of their trades with the help of a trading journal. When you keep a trading journal, you ensure that you are keeping track of your experiences in the market so that you can come back to them later for lessons.

When you develop a trading journal/system, the most important thing is to save ideas in then and then test results. In other words, when you enter a certain position, you simply need to record everything about the trade. Ensure that you capture all your thoughts and contemplations when making a trade. This means that when you later have a "what was I thinking" moment in the future, all your answers will be found in the journal.

When setting up a trading journal, ensure that it has the following; trade date, number of shares and the reason you chose them, stock symbol, whether they are sold long/short, what triggered the entry signal and exit signal, where was your initial stop, did you move your stops and why, what was the reasons for your exit position?

Also, when you set up the trading journal, it is important that you keep track of not just your trades but beyond. For instance, the internet articles that influenced your thoughts, what the leading and lagging industries were and the charts that helped you through the process.

Even though keeping a journal is key, it is critical if you regularly review it. Therefore, set aside some time each week or month to just go through your trades to identify key mistakes and missed opportunities. Ensure that you are brutally honest with yourself by simply stepping back, taking a cold and hard look at the decisions you made when trading.

In short, your trading journal should be the soil that nurtures your growth.

Chapter 8: Money Management

What Is Money Management?

This term is used to refer to the process of investing, spending, saving, and budgeting; it is also used to refer to the way capital is used for personal or group usage. The other words used for money management includes portfolio and investment management. When you are good with money, it involves a lot apart from just meeting your needs. When it comes to money management, having math skills is not mandatory, there are different skills needed that will be discussed later.

Money management is simply how you handle all the finances and how you handle all your long-term goals. It also involves how an individual manages their investment in order to make great profits. Most people think that great money management skills are all about saying no when you are tempted to make a purchase. What it really implies is when you are able to say yes to what is important to purchase. When you do not practice good money management skills, whatever money you have might look little for your lifestyle.

To have a good start when it comes to money management, you need to know where you are. This is in terms of your financial capability and power; like assets and liabilities. Assets include your investment and bank accounts, any properties and retirement accounts. Liabilities are the things that you need to pay like credit card balances, any loans like student loans and car loans and any mortgages and outstanding debts. Your net worth is when the value of your assets is more than your liabilities. And when your liabilities are more than your asset that is considered a net loss or negative net worth. When you have great money management skills and approaches, getting a net worth will be easy.

Ensure that you set your goals in order to achieve great money management. Your goals will create a plan on how you will manage your money. When you have your goals set, it will give clarity on which are priority expenses and which you can let go. You will need discipline and effort in order to achieve all your efforts. For instance, when you plan to buy a car worth $20k, you will need to work harder and smarter and reduce your expenses. You will need to do all that as compared to someone whose budget car is $10k.

When you have your budget drafted and set, remember to have adjustments. When you prepare a budget, you have the chance to know all the expenses that you have. For instance, you can set aside $150 that can be for entertainment and any miscellaneous expenses after payment of all expenses and managing your debts. Good advice is when you get a pay increment, do not use the additional income for your entertainment but add it into your savings.

When you have a target to meet different goals, you are likely to have the money in different multiple accounts. A good example will be to ensure that you have a separate emergency fund so as not to get tempted for any impulse buying in the future. You will also have different strategies and that will be for different goals. You will be aggressive when you start investing in different stocks that you will not need to invest money in like 20 years. You need to also have an account that has no risks like a savings account that that can be used as emergency funds when the need arises. When you have such multiple accounts, you can use a software program to help in tracking the several accounts. A good one can be Quicken; it will track all your expenses and the savings goals.

The Basics of Money Management

Money management is a term that deals with solutions and services that are in the investment field. The good thing is, in the financial market there are different resources available that can help in personal financial management. For any investor, their intention is to have a good net worth, so it will come a time when they will need the services of professionals like financial advisors. The advisors are known to offer brokerage services, money management plans, and private banking. The advice is best for retirement, estate planning and other benefits.

When you are in business, it seems complicated when there is a need to manage cash flow and different accounts. When you are able to strike a balance, you are guaranteed to be successful. If you are not able to manage all that, you will need to get the services of an accountant or bookkeeper to do all that for you. Even if you will outsource, you need to know the basics of money management and bookkeeping. You will need to know simple tasks like interpreting bank statements, understanding accounts payable and receivable, credit, and tax forms.

Money management will also involve knowing more about debit cards, checks, online payments, cash, and credit cards when it comes to payment options in your business. You will also need to have a planned and established payment plan and a debt collection system just in case of non-payment.

Opening a bank account is another way to help in money management, you need to choose a name and have an operating and registered business. Make sure you get more information on credit card facilities, a debit account, and any other additional services. Another important concept is to ensure that you have extended credit facilities in case of late payments. This can be planned for 30-6-90-120 days after a product is delivered or a service is rendered. You can motivate your customers to pay on time by extending discounts. Before the credit extension, ensure that you have done proper background check especially with large amounts. Even when there is credit extension, there are times where you will end up not being paid or not aid in time. To be able to recover your money, you need to ensure there is open and clear communication.

What Are Money Management Skills?

Before you can know of the best skills for money management, you will need to ask yourself some questions. What is your weekly or monthly income? Do you have a list of expenses that you need to pay? What you need to know is that money management is a skill used in life and cannot be taught in school. These skills cannot be learned in school but mostly from life experience.

✓ Have the ability to set a budget. This will help in tracking your expenses and the way you spend money. What do you spend a lot on, is it entertainment, clothes, or food? What is the tendency of overdrawing money from your bank account? If all that is yes, then you will need to set a budget. Look at your monthly statement and write down all the expenses in categories. You will be surprised by how much you are wasting.

✓ Spend what you have wisely. Always have a shopping list when you go shopping. Do you have a habit of looking at the product prices before putting it in the shopping basket? If you have coupons, ensure you use them. There are mobile apps and online resources that can help in focusing on your expenses. Do you know how to monitor your expenses? When you are not attentive to this advice, you will end up losing your hard-earned money.

✓ Always balance your books, do not always have a tendency of getting your bank balance online. When you depend on online information, there will be an issue when you want to know the balance on what you are spending at that particular moment. Be accountable and ensure you record all your expenses and this will help in avoiding any over-spending.

✓ Set a plan that will help in accomplishing anything that you put your mind. When you have a financial plan, you will be able to track how you are spending your money.

✓ Always think like an investor. When in school, you will not be taught how to handle money but largely on how to invest your money and have wealth growth. Learn to grow your savings and to invest at an early age. Turn that $100 to $200, $400, $800, and more. Having a stable financial future means that you have invested and grown in your money. When you start thinking like an investor, your money will grow. If you have a spouse or partner ensure that, they also know about your financial goals. If you possess a joint account with your partner or spouse, always work together and agree on the financial goals. When you are stuck or in doubt, consult a financial adviser and learn a lot of how to invest.

✓ Save your money, always be focused, and committed when it comes to saving money and this will guarantee a better future. This will help in improving your financial position and even make it better. The first step is to have the decision to do that and this will help improve your management skills.

Importance of Money Management

Money management will help any individual in living on a budget and within their means. You will be able to look for great bargains and avoid any deals you believe that is not good when making a purchase. When you start getting a stable income, you will need to know how to invest because that will help in attaining your goals. And when you practice proper money management, you will meet all your goals and plans. There is the importance of money management:

✓ You will have better financial security: When you are careful with your expenses and savings, you will end up having enough for your future. Your savings will help in giving the proper financial security and you will be able to take care of yourself in case of emergencies. With your savings, you will not need to use your credit card in case of any issues.

✓ When you have proper money management and manage to save, you will be able to get opportunities and invest in the business. It will be frustrating to know of a great opportunity and not having enough funds to invest.

- ✓ Your credit scores will be determined by the way you manage your money. When you have high credit, score means you have managed to pay your bills on time and you have low-level debt. A high credit score means you will have more savings and you will be charged low interest when making purchases like cars or mortgages.

- ✓ Money management helps in reducing stress, this will happen when you start paying your bills on time. When you are late in paying your bills, you will encounter stress. Stress will bring about health problems like insomnia, migraines, and hypertension. You need to be aware of how you will handle money management, this will help in having extra cash and manage to save and manage a stress-free life.

- ✓ Money management helps in earning more money and when your income increases, you need to develop proper budgeting. And know of the right places to invest the extra money you have made. You need to know of additional venues to save money like in stocks and mutual funds; this will help in earning more money unlike money laying in your savings account. Ensure you learn about the investments, not all investments are profitable. The better thing about investments is that you can be on a monthly salary and still earning from your investment.

✓ When you adapt great money management skills, you will not waste money on unnecessary things. When you do not know how you are spending your income, it will be easy to be in debt. When you use your spare time effectively, it will help in managing your money. For instance, when you spend time with your friends and family members, ensure that you are aware of your budget.

✓ Peace of mind is guaranteed when you have better money management skills. When you a stable income and better savings, you will be able to handle any financial issues with confidence that all your needs can be handled perfectly.

World Top Money Managers

These managers are known to offer management and investment advice. They manage both active and passive funds.

✓ The Vanguard Group: It is a well-known management and investment firm, they have more than 20 million clients and in more than 100 countries. They started in Pennsylvania in the '70s and they have grown their assets to more than $5 trillion by close of 2018. They hold over 300 funds, move 150 in the US and more than 400 indexes to all of their market funds.

✓ Pacific Investment Management Company: This management firm has a worldwide presence and founded in California in the '70s. They have grown their asset base to more than $1 trillion by close of 2018. They have over 700 professional managing investments and with over 10 years as experts. They have over 100 funds and they lead in the fixed income sector.

- ✓ BlackRock, Inc: They started with their main company as BlackRock Group, by 1988 they started another division and labeled it BlackRock, Inc. They grew their assets to over $15 billion in 5 years and by the end of 2018, they grew to over $6 trillion and they have become the largest company in investment management in the world. They have over 100k in their workforce and over 50 offices in more than 30 countries. More than 20% of their assets are equivalent to $16 trillion.

- ✓ Fidelity Investments: This firm was founded in the '40s and by end of 2019 their customers have grown to over 20 million and more than $5 trillion in asset base. Their mutual fund is more than 300, this includes domestic and foreign equity, money market, fixed income, money markets and allocation of funds.

- ✓ Invesco Ltd: This firm has been in business since 1940 in offering investment advice. They announced in 2018, that they have made over $800 billion way above their products. They have over 100 EFTs that are made from their share capital. In 2017, they had a decline and it affected their stock price. They have managed to be among the best in the world despite all the challenges and setbacks. They have become among the top and best companies in the world, in terms of money, assets, and investment management.

The Approaches Used in Money Management

Great financial skills make money management easier, and how our money is spent largely affects your credit score and your debt cycle. There are tips that can help you if you are struggling with how to manage your money.

✓ Always have a Budget: Most people do not like to have a budget because they believe it is a boring and repetitive process. That involves listing all their expenses, summing up numbers, getting everything up, and running. When you have a budget, there is less room to be bad with money. You will get to know your income and expenses. The secret is focusing on the value that the budget will bring to your life instead of the budget creation process.

✓ After making the budget, the trick is to make sure that you use your budget. It will be a waste of time when you draft a budget and you do not stick to it. If it is a weekly or monthly budget, ensure that you refer to it often, and it will help when making your spending decisions. The budget should be made in a way that, at any given time you can easily track how much you have spent and know of any penning expenses.

✓ When drafting your budget, have a limit set for any unbudgeted expenses. In any budget, what is important to know is the funds left after paying all your expenses. When you have any budget and everything is settled, you can have the balance for your entertainment purposes. The amount set for fun should be a specific amount from your income. If you are planning to have a big purchase, refer to your budget first.

✓ Start by tracking your spending habits. When you have small purchases, they will end up piling and finally, you will notice that you have gone beyond your budget. When you track your spending plans. you will be able to know the places that you are failing and how you can rectify them. If you can, ensure that you save all your receipts and have a record of your spending in a journal. Have them in categories so that you can easily track them and know of the areas that are hard to stick on a budget.

✓ When your income is steady and qualifies you for a credit facility that does not mean that you should get that facility. You do not need to commit yourself to any monthly recurring bill. Most people think that the bank will not approve of the facility because they cannot afford it. What the bank knows is just your income exactly as you have reported. And if you have given a credit report, they will use what is offered on that report and they will not have any obligations not to give the credit facility. It is a personal decision to know if you qualify for the credit facility and if you have the capability to pay regarding your monthly income and other obligations.

✓ When making a purchase decision, ensure that you are paying the right and best prices. The best way to do this is by making a comparison and making sure that you are paying the lowest prices for the products and any services rendered. Look for discounts, cheaper alternatives, and coupons.

✓ In situations whereby you are planning to make a huge purchase, ensure that you save for that purchase. When you have the ability to delay gratification, will help in ensuring that you manage your money in a better way. It is advisable to out of large purchases, instead of sacrificing important things or tying a purchase to a credit card. This will help in evaluating if you really need the purchase or more time to do a price comparison. Ensure that you develop a habit of saving up instead of having a tendency to use credit cards; this will help in avoiding any interest on the cost price.

✓ Always limit the purchases that you do use your credit card. In situations whereby you run out of cash, chances are that you will end up using your credit card even if you cannot even afford the purchase and paying the balance. Learn to resist from using your credit cards when making any purchases that you know you cannot afford and especially on this that you do not need.

✓ Develop a habit of saving regularly. Open a savings account and ensure that you deposit money regularly; you can do it daily, weekly, or monthly depending on your income. This will definitely help in developing a healthier financial habit. Another better way will be to set up a plan that the funds are automatically credited to your account. That will help reduce the responsibility of reminding yourself to do that all the time.

- ✓ If you need to be a good manager when it comes to money, ensure that you practice it all the time. Plan when you intend to make a purchase and always buy what you can afford. When you make it a routine and a daily habit, it will be easier to manage money and the better for your finances.

Money Market Mistakes

To be successful in your investment in the money market, you need to ask yourself several questions/statements:

1. *<u>Do you have an account for emergencies?</u>*
2. *<u>The account that you have will be an investment</u>*
3. *<u>That the funds you are setting aside will be useful soon.</u>*

When you decide to invest, you need to know that it is a risky venture and there are factors that you will need to consider first before any investment. For instance, when you decide to invest in a stock you need to know of factors like economic volatility. In the case of bonds, there are challenges like interest rates and inflationary risks. For a brave investor, leaning on a money market account will be a brave move. This is because they are known for safekeeping for the money. There are several mistakes when it comes to money market:

✓   The mistake that most investors make is thinking that money market accounts are the same as money market funds. They are financial instruments that have distinctive differences. Most people know of the money market fund as a mutual fund, the main characteristics are low returns and risks for every investment. They invest their funds in liquid assets for example cash. When invested in debt securities they have higher returns and ratings and mature in a shorter time. Most investors make the mistake and think that their money is safer in the money market, but that is not the same as with money market funds.

✓   Most people who are in investment believe that the money that they have in the money market is safe. The biggest mistake that they make is thinking that they are even safer from investments. Another belief is that, it better to have a lower interest rate with money in the bank than no interest at all. Most investors do not know the exposure they are in regarding inflation. This is the main reason that funds that are in the money market will not beat inflation. A good example is when the inflation rate is low than the interest that is claimed. Investors would know that, even though they believe the money market is safe, they are not safe from inflation.

✓   When in investment, you always need to know how to strike the right balance. Most of the time, the money market is influenced by inflation changes and rates. When you have such an investment, do not be tempted to input higher capital. They need a higher minimum balance as compared to the normal savings accounts. The normal account needs to be in operation for at least one year and have a higher amount of capital. When you have anything more than that, then it will be sitting their idle and it will lose value.

✓   Most investors like using money as their safety blanket. They believe that when they hold onto their money, it will be the best approach for any investment. This is not true especially when it is about savings whether in their money market or standard savings. It is not right to have your money exposed to uncertainty and any risk. This is one of the reasons why investors are afraid to invest and they would rather stay with their cash.

✓ To be a good investor, you need to know about asset diversification. When you are dealing with cash that is no different at all; this is because most people believe that cash is not an asset. You need to know that from the basics of finance and accounting, cash is known as a current asset. When you decide to hold on cash, ensure you do not hold more than $200k. It is not a coincidence to find any ordinary investor who has several bank accounts, in order to secure their cash. They have an approach to divide money or cash into three categories and that is a useful thing. The first one is to ensure that you have some money set aside for at least 3 years that is considered a shorter period. Around 4 to 10 years as the average timeframe and above 10 years as the longest timeframe. This is what will help the investors to know how long they can time their projects, how much is needed, and what will be saved in the end. This approach is important because it will also help in knowing about all the risks.

The best advice is to ensure that you invest in investments that are in the long-term and on lower risks. These will include investments like bonds, treasury bonds, life insurance, and annuity. You will need to know of the options that will help to avoid losing money value, avoiding any risks and the different ways about cash diversification. You can make use of the different trading and investment tools that will help in giving more returns instead of money market accounts. You need to look for investments that will help in creating more returns in a shorter time than the longer timeframe.

✓ Any investor needs to know that the reason for the money market is to hold money. When you have your money in just one place, you will not have any earnings or benefits; you need to move the money around. You will need to get more information on the different options and invest more. You should also know that money market accounts are not to be considered as long-term investments. The main reason is that they are subject to high interest rates than what is charged on a normal savings account. Hence not the reason to consider it a long-term investment.

✓ You should not be enticed to look for accounts that offer interest rates as a promotion. The reason is the interests are bound to change after some time.

Budgeting Apps

As an investor, you need to know that, with the tough economic times you need to know the best way to invest in the financial market. And when you become successful and start making money, you need to look for apps that will in managing your money. Thanks to technology all, those apps are easily available and easy to download. They can be downloaded and installed on tablets and smartphones; hence you can use them anytime and anywhere you are due to portability. The apps help is keeping you on track regarding the way you spend and how you spend.

✓ MINT:

Mint can be downloaded as an app or used as a website; it is in the budgeting and investment category. It is compatible with iOS, Web, Windows 8, and Android. It is more of a budgeting app and it will still help in managing your money. It has a feature whereby you can categorize and customize all your expenses and transactions. It has the ability to synchronize all your transactions from investments, bank accounts, and credit cards. They have a reminder feature for all your pending bills and this helps to avoid any lateness in bill payment that should be very convenient for any investor. All you need to do is set up a free account and then include all your financial details. This will then give a breakdown anytime an activity happens and you will be able to get a report.

- [x] **Good Budget:**

This app uses the envelope concept, when you sign up you are given 10 free envelopes when you are on standard subscription. When you have an upgrade to Plus, you will then be charged a monthly charge of $6, and then you will have unlimited envelopes. The concept works in a way that, when your envelope is empty, you are not able to shop or spend any money. The other alternative is that you can move money among envelopes; this is because the app has the flexibility to use a common budget. You can share the budget with other people, the app is compatible with iPhone and all android devices.

- [x] Dollar Bird:

This app also helps in money management; it manages future expenses and will remind you when you have payment dues. To set up and activate is free and it has additional premium features. Your budget will be broken down in a calendar form and your pending expenses will be visible. You have the chance to have all your transactions in categories that are color-coded and they will keep on adding up as you have repeated transactions. When you check on your utility bill and paycheck, they will be displayed there. You will be able to see all your current balance. What you can spend and still be on a budget. The main setback is that it does not synchronize will your bank accounts. The problem is you will need to manually enter all the transactions. The app is available for iOS users, Android, and the web. You will have the privilege to know about your income, expenses, and cash flow.

✓ **EXPENSIFY:**

This is considered an app and tool that is used to report expenses, track all receipts, and all the expenses that you have. The main advantage is that it helps in quick data entry and saves a lot of time doing data entry. You will have the opportunity to make all the entries in one click. This app is available for Android and iOS users, you will do all the capturing automatically and using OCR; this is a smart scan. All your reports are available by taking one picture and they are all uploaded and completed within a click. When you submit your expense, they get reimbursed faster and approvals are done very fast. When you use the app, you will be able to track all your expenses, categorize all of them, know the cost of all. All the expenses are consolidated and synchronized.

Chapter 9: Risk and Account Management

Risk management is a deliberate action taken by a trader or investor. The purpose is to keep losses at a minimum. As a trader, you are exposed to a lot of dangers. You can lose money if you are not careful or if your strategy was not successful. Should you lose money in a trade, then the risk can be managed. All that you need to do is to open yourself up to being profitable in the market.

Most traders are unaware of risk management yet it is a crucial aspect of any serious trader. If you wish to make money in the markets for the long term, then risk management is absolutely essential. Even if you are a great trader and profitable most of the time, your profits can be wiped out in a matter of seconds without proper risk management.

As a trader, you really need to incorporate risk management as part of your trading strategy. There are a number of different approaches to risk management, so it is advisable to consider the approach that best works for you.

Risk management is a grossly neglected area of every unsuccessful trader's strategy. Indeed, most do not even understand the concept and fail to explore it beyond the cursory nod given to stop losses and per trade risk.

Perfect risk management can save a poor strategy but even the best strategy cannot save poor risk management. Many of you must have heard of this piece of wisdom but probably very few of you truly understand its implications.

Risk in trading is quite simple. It is the probability of you losing your capital on a series of trades, including the current one.

Plan Your Trades

Some of the best tools you will need as part of your risk management plan are take-profit and stop-loss. Using these two tools, you can plan your trades in advance. You will need to use technical analysis in order to determine these two points. With this information, you should be able to determine the price you are willing to pay as well as the losses you can incur.

Adhere to a Proven Trading Method

Furthermore, do not transform it. In the event that you have a demonstrated technique however it does not appear to work in a given exchanging session, do not return home that night and attempt to devise another. In the event that your strategy works for more than one-portion of the exchanging sessions, at that point stay with it. Keep in mind, the Holy Grail of exchanging is cashing the executives.

Consistency is Confidence

How great does it feel have the option to turn on your exchanging stage the morning realizing that, on the off chance that you play by the guidelines, the likelihood of fruitful exchanging day is generally high? The appropriate response? Great! Keep in mind: If you make somewhat consistently, at that point you have earned the privilege to exchange greater.

Try not to Chase the Markets

Proficient merchants that pick Admiral Markets will be satisfied to realize that they can exchange totally chance free with a FREE demo exchanging account. Rather than going to the live markets and putting your capital in danger, you can dodge the hazard out and out and essentially practice until you are prepared to change to live exchanging.

Pursue Your Trading Routine

Never attempt to break your exchanging schedule. Pursue real markets and exchange just during the significant markets. These include: New York, London and Tokyo markets. The value moves all the more detectably during significant market sessions, so you can disregard minor markets. Significant markets furnish you with an incredible number of arrangements as well.

Maintaining a trading Journal

You can do this online or keep a paper copy nearby. When you are done with one trade, make sure to write down what happened during that trade, what strategy you used, what was going on in the market, how much you spent, and more.

If you ever get stuck with one of your trades or you aren't sure how to handle one situation or another, you can refer back to this journal and see what advice it has. You may be surprised that, after a particularly hard situation in a different trade, you can look back in this journal and find the answers that you need. More than anything else, your trade journal is what will keep your risk management on track. Your journal should, at a minimum, record your trade date, instrument, direction (long or short), stop loss size, reasons for entering, exit date, P/L and any comments.

As a trader, you need to keep a journal so that you have a reliable record of your trades and their performance. This is one of the best ways of learning about your style and performance. Trade tracking journals also enables you to track your trades and the actions you took during certain situations and instances. In short, a trading journal provides traders with the necessary tools and information that they need to evaluate their trading activities objectively.

As a trader, you really should be tracking your trades throughout the day. A journal helps you to keep a record of the happenings each day as well as your reactions or actions. Your plan should include a tried and tested system that suits your trading style. Make sure that you test this system and review it often then improve your trading plans and performance.

Setting Target and Stops

We can define a stop-loss as the total amount of loss that a trader is willing to incur in a single trade. Beyond the stop-loss point, the trader exits the trade. This is basically meant to prevent further losses by thinking the trade will eventually get some momentum. We also have what is known as a take-profit point. It is at this point that you will collect any profits made and possibly exit a trade. At this point, a particular stock or other security is often very close to the point of resistance. Beyond this point, a reversal in price is likely to take place. Rather than lose money, you should exit the trade. Traders sometimes take profit and let a particular trade continue if it was still making money. Another take-profit point is then plotted. If you have a good run, you are allowed to lock in the profits and let the good run continue.

Assessing Risk versus Reward

A lot of traders tend to think of the outcome of their trade in terms of the amount they make, that is, $100 or -$50 and so on. This is a warped way of thinking since it places an undue amount of importance on the amount of money one makes. This is not to say it's unimportant but the best way to make money trading isn't in following this method.

Instead, you need to measure the outcome of your trades as a function of your risk per trade, that is, as a multiple of your R (R being the percent of your capital you risk per trade). Thus on a loss, your profit/loss record (P/L) will read -R and on a win your P/L will read 1.5R or 2R and so on. Recording it this way puts the focus squarely on your risk management and forces you to think in terms of risk.

A lot of traders lose a lot of money at the markets for a very simple reason. They do not know about risk management or how to go about it. This mostly happens to beginners or novice traders. Most of them simply learn how to trade then rush to the markets in the hope of making a kill. Sadly, this is now how things work because account and risk management are not taken into consideration.

Think about it this way. Supposing someone you don't trust many approaches you for a $1,000 loan with a promise to pay you back with $100 interest after a month. You may be hesitant because the risk is greater compared than the profit. However, if he promises to pay you back after one month with a $2,000 interest, then the risk is well worth it. The ratio of risk versus reward, in this case, is 2:1. A lot of investors believe this to be an excellent ratio and many would take it because they get a chance to double their money. If the borrower offered to pay back $3,000, then the risk vs. reward ratio increases to 3:1.

A trader who is unsuccessful will likely look at an entry and then only think about the profit they will make on that trade. But, a trader who is successful is always going to consider the upside and the downside with any trade they choose. So, they are going to think about how much of a risk they are going to have if they take a loss. It is all about comparing the amount of risk that you are going to take to the reward that you are hoping to get from that trade.

For the reward, they are hoping that the XBI stock is going to reach $91.00 for each share or the prior area of resistance. This can help them earn $3.50 a share for this one. This means that, in this scenario, the risk is $1.00 a share, but the reward is a potential $3.50 a share. This ends up being a very good risk to reward ratio. If the reward only ended up being $0.75 a share, then it is best to look for another option since the risk is too high for that trade.

Always ensure to apply the risk versus reward ratio for all your trades. Keep in mind the indicated acceptable levels. If you are unable to find acceptable ratios after trying several times, find another security. Once you learn how to incorporate risk management into your trades, you will become safer as you trade without incurring any huge losses.

Managing the Trade Size

As a trader, you also need to make determinations regarding other aspects of the trade. These include the number of stock or currency or any other financial markets' instruments. When doing this, most traders overlook position size. They feel like it is not important enough or sometimes they have no clue that it is necessary and how to determine an optimum one.

Some traders have large accounts and wish they could spend freely. These usually employ different approaches when it comes to position size. Even if you had an account worth $500,000, then you would not want to risk over $500 per trade. This is equivalent to 1% of the total amount in the account.

Sometimes, people choose stop levels for the day. These are daily stop orders issued by a client to their broker and so on. Daily stop-loss points simply indicate the amount of money that you are ready to lose per trade. Should this level be attained as you trade, then you will have to stop trading and exit all other possible positions in the market.

Experienced traders usually opt to equate the daily stop-loss positions as equivalent to their average profitability. So if a person makes $400, then their stop loss order will be a lot closer to this figure.

Keep Your Emotions in Check

Keeping your emotions in check is especially important when you find a stock going against you. Not only does this make you realize that you made a mistake during your analysis and any calculations, which carries its own emotions, but this can also make you go through a series of emotional stages. There are many traders and investors who state that this series of five stages is similar to the five stages of grief.

 Follow the 1% Rule

One of the biggest ways to reduce your risk is to make sure that you focus on keeping your proportion low. One of the best ways to do this is to only risk about 1% of the money in your account with each trade. For example, if you have $10,000 in your account, this means that you will not trade more than $100 on a trade. However, many expert swing traders believe that when you are first starting out, you should lower this even more. Therefore, a beginner should look at trading no more than around 0.3% to 0.5%. While this doesn't seem like a lot of money, most stocks generally aren't a large amount of money to buy. Some of the most expensive stocks to buy will be blue-chip stocks.

Determine a Stop-Loss Amount

After you have looked at setting your risk at 1%, you can look at another factor, which is setting your trade risk. This is when you set your stop-loss amount. This amount will be created when you set up your trading plan. For example, if you spent $10.00 on your trade, then you might set up your stop-loss level at $9.80. This means that once you reach this amount, you will sell that stock and only lose .20 cents. Most traders will look at the percentage of their account they put towards their stock in order to help them determine their stop-loss amount. This is because some traders might feel more comfortable setting their stop-loss amount at a higher percentage if they followed the 1% rule than an if they decided to go up to 3% or even 5%.

Follow Your Guidelines and Rules

As you get started in your trading career, you will start to develop your own rules and guidelines, such as in your trading plan. It is important that you don't change any of these rules and guidelines without fully looking at your trade as a whole. On top of this, it is important to follow because it will help keep you focused, you will begin to learn the details of swing trading easier as you won't be so concerned about your next step, and you will feel more comfortable in your abilities.

Conclusion

It's important to remember that this book is not meant to stand in for the role of a financial adviser, nor is it meant to provide investment or tax advice. We are proving this information as a resource for you to consider when making your own financial investment decisions.

Past performance does not indicate future outcomes, nor does its analysis prevent risk of loss. Investing, whether long-term, swing, or day trade, requires risk taking and always involved the potential loss of assets/capital.

Last but not least, like always, make a plan and stick to it. Day trading more than any other type of trading requires proper planning and diligence. Your trading plan is how you're going to make money. Deviate from it and you'll get lost in the weeds before you even realize it. Decide your position size, psychology, and handful of strategies before delving in full time. When the market decides to play a few tricks on you, you'll be glad that you were prepared.

Swing and day trading are the practices of getting the stock market to work for you. It does all of the heavy lifting, and you reap the benefits. The first step is to decide what type of trader you want to be, and what your style is. Then you can decide on the important things: your broker, your trading platform, the size of your positions, and your favorite strategy. We hope this book has given you advanced tips on swing trading and a base from which to start day trading. We've also tried to prepare you with the knowledge of how to pick strategies based on risk and reward, and how day trading strategies will change the way you schedule your life. You've also been taught how to evaluate risk, position size, and competition in day trading. We're confident that you're going to make some steps along the way to becoming an advanced swing trader or day trader. But that's the essential key. We can't teach you everything. If there's one thing that we hope this book does for you, is make you want to go out there and practice, practice, practice! That's the only way. As you learned early on in your trading days, separate your emotions from your trading, learn your lessons, and keep going.

© Copyright 2020 - All rights reserved.

The content contained within this book may not be reproduced, duplicated or transmitted without direct written permission from the author or the publisher.

Under no circumstances will any blame or legal responsibility be held against the publisher, or author, for any damages, reparation, or monetary loss due to the information contained within this book. Either directly or indirectly.

Legal Notice:
This book is copyright protected. This book is only for personal use. You cannot amend, distribute, sell, use, quote or paraphrase any part, or the content within this book, without the consent of the author or publisher.

Disclaimer Notice:
Please note the information contained within this document is for educational and entertainment purposes only. All effort has been executed to present accurate, up to date, and reliable, complete information. No warranties of any kind are declared or implied. Readers acknowledge that the author is not engaging in the rendering of legal, financial, medical or professional advice. The content within this book has been derived from various sources. Please consult a licensed professional before attempting any techniques outlined in this book.

By reading this document, the reader agrees that under no circumstances is the author responsible for any losses, direct or indirect, which are incurred as a result of the use of information contained within this document, including, but not limited to, — errors, omissions, or inaccuracies.